The Big Bake Sale Cookbook

Barbara C. Jones

Published by Cookbook Resources, LLC
Highland Village, Texas

The Big Bake Sale Cookbook

1st Printing   January 2007

ISBN: 978-1-931294-49-2
Library of Congress Number: 2007900001

Illustrations by Nancy Bohanan

Edited, Designed and Published in the
United States of America
Manufactured in China

Cookbook Resources, LLC
541 Doubletree Drive
Highland Village, Texas 75077
Toll free 866-229-2665
www.cookbookresources.com

The Best Source For Easy Cookbooks

cookbook resources LLC
The Ultimate Source for Easy Cookbooks

Introduction

Bake sales are wonderful ways to raise funds for schools, religious organizations and community clubs. Individuals contribute their own time and resources to provide the freshest, tastiest inventory possible to raise funds for their group.

This is where **The Big Bake Sale Cookbook** comes to the rescue. No one wants to show up at a bake sale with another ho-hum item and "hope it sells". Lucky for you, this cookbook is filled with yummy, tempting treats that are sure to sell fast (if you can keep from eating them first).

This wonderful collection of bake sale recipes includes the best of bars, breads, candy, cakes, cookies, muffins and pies.

Included are bake sale tips for packaging, tagging, naming, greeting, transporting and selling.

If you have a bake sale question, The Big Bake Sale Cookbook has the answer!

Contents

Bake Sale Tips

Bake sales are wonderful ways to raise funds for non-profit organizations and school groups. How you plan, organize and display a bake sale can be the difference between selling some cakes to the neighbors and conducting a successful community fundraiser. Here are some tips, ideas and shortcuts to increase traffic, sales and encourage repeat business for bake sales to come.

Plan Plan Plan

Where? When?
Select a time, date, place for your bake sale. You first want to compare your selected date against competing sales on your community calendar. Remember factors such as weather, traffic, pedestrian traffic and community events when planning your bake sale.

Don't go at it alone.
A bake sale raises funds for an organization. Organize your team and rely on responsible people to carry through their tasks. Have plenty of volunteers for baking. Assign a small task force for advertising, marketing and decorations. Have each member of your organization find a "buddy" to bake as well.

Gather materials in advance.
Attempting to find several matching tablecloths or folding tables the morning of a bake sale will not help your cause. Look for good buys and gather items ahead of time. Pick your theme early on. When you see items that will suit your sale's theme, go ahead and get them.

Materials you will need include:
Tables and Chairs
Calculator
Cash box (with change!)
Napkins and Cups
Gloves (if anyone will be handling unwrapped food)
Price tags, labels, markers and pens
Beverage Containers (Thermos, Ice Chest, Etc)
Bottled Water (for sale)

Preparation and Advertising:

Community newspapers are wonderful resources for organizations hosting a bake sale. By typing up a short, clever press release, you are gaining an advertising edge. Make sure to include, date, time, location and a sample of what will be available to purchase. The best part -- news stories are free advertising! Remember to write a "letter to the editor" or publisher thanking them for their local support.

Sample press release:

NEWS RELEASE
FOR IMMEDIATE RELEASE

CONTACT:
[Your Name]
[Phone number including area code]

Good taste is on display at [Name or organization or fundraiser title] Bake Sale.

[Your City] – Cakes, breads, candy and cookies are available [day, time] only! Volunteers for [name of organization] are baking various selections of tasty treats for their upcoming bake sale at [location]. The [group, association] will have delectable treats such as [list at least three different kinds of desserts that you plan on having].

[Use this space to let your community know what the proceeds will be used for and thank them for their upcoming support].

Find a business that is willing to match or double your proceeds. Large grocery stores, discount centers or local markets usually have a community budget to donate to your cause.

Flyers

Simple, bright, inviting flyers can be worth a pound cake's weight in gold. Design flyers on your home or office computer. Call local copy-shops. Explain that your bake sale is a fundraiser for your organization. Local "mom and pop" shops might even be kind enough to donate the photocopied flyers.

Distribute the flyers to local businesses, radio and television stations, schools and around neighborhoods. Send a sample of goodies to the radio and television stations. One taste and they will sing your praises to an audience that only the media can reach.

Marketing

Allow advanced orders. Who says you can only sell on one day? If you had customers last year that will not be in town or are busy on your bake sale day, let them place orders in advance. Even offer to deliver the items (where cost effective). Include a flyer when delivering pre-ordered goods.

Talk to your local radio station about sponsoring the event with an on-site remote. If the station's schedule permits, you might get free radio advertising and entertainment rolled into one package!

Sell it!

You can't just cook and look. Dress up every item. Display your baked goods on decorative platters, inside colored plastic wrap; use bows, ribbons and note cards. Explain what each item is, include ingredients and suggest ways this cake or candy could be a great gift.

Offer a sample plate of small pieces of a variety of items available at the sale. Nothing speaks to a wallet better than a hungry tummy. Don't forget to have drinks available. Coffee, sodas or juice can be great ways to raise additional funds.

Offer single-serving selections. Some people really don't need an entire cake. Be sure to price the single servings in a way that they are still cost effective.

Use decorations. Balloons, tablecloths and ribbons are fun, inexpensive ways to draw the customer in. Keep the colors simple. You don't want to overpower the look of the fresh, baked items.
Make a basket of select items. Hold a raffle for that particular basket. Just don't give away the basket until its time to wrap up the sale. The Holiday Lemon-Pecan Cake is an excellent choice for a raffle item. Because of the extra cost associated with its ingredients, you won't lose money or be forced to charge a higher price for one item.

Have plenty of table space. A cluttered table is distracting. Easy shopping makes way for easy buying.

If possible, turn your bake sale into a social event with live music, food demonstrations, games or a clown (balloon-animal guy will work here too). Make it special. Inform your guests that this is sure to become a community tradition.

Hold the bake sale around a holiday. Find seasonal items to use as decoration.

Include a "thank you" note with each purchase. On this note, remind the buyer where their money went and why it is so important to support community fundraisers such as this particular bake sale. They will be back year after year.

Branch out! Offering your sale at two or more locations can only help matters. The more ground you cover, the more money you make.

BAKE SALE
TODAY

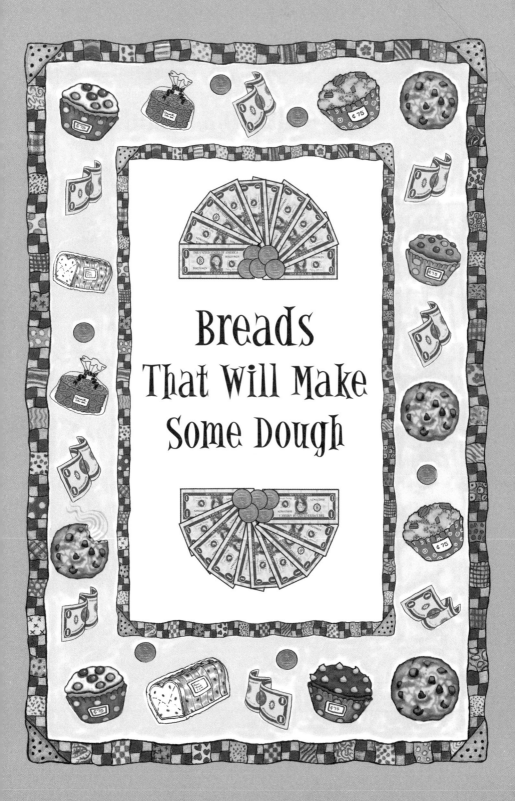

Breads
That Will Make
Some Dough

Apple-Banana Bread

3 apples, peeled, grated	
3 bananas, mashed	
2 teaspoons lemon juice	10 ml
½ cup (1 stick) butter, softened	120 ml
2 cups sugar	480 ml
2 eggs	
3 cups flour	710 ml
1½ teaspoons baking powder	7 ml
1½ teaspoons baking soda	7 ml
1 teaspoon vanilla	5 ml

- Preheat oven to 350° (176° C).

- Sprinkle apples and bananas with lemon juice. In mixing bowl, cream butter, sugar and eggs and beat well.

- Stir in fruit. Add dry ingredients and ⅓ teaspoon (3 ml) salt and vanilla and stir.

- Pour into 2 (9 x 5-inch/23 x 13 cm) sprayed, floured loaf pans and bake for 50 to 55 minutes or until golden brown. Bread is done when toothpick inserted in center comes out clean.

Banana Bread

1 cup sugar	240 ml
2 eggs, beaten	
½ cup shortening, melted	120 ml
3 tablespoons sour cream	45 ml
2 cups flour	480 ml
1 teaspoon baking powder	5 ml
3 bananas, mashed	

- Preheat oven to 325° (162° C).

- Beat sugar and eggs and add slightly cooled, melted shortening. Stir in sour cream, flour, baking powder and mashed bananas. Pour into sprayed, floured loaf pan. Bake for 1 hour.

Applesauce-Pecan Bread

1 cup sugar	240 ml
1 cup applesauce	240 ml
⅓ cup oil	80 ml
2 eggs	
2 tablespoons milk	30 ml
1 teaspoon almond extract	5 ml
2 cups flour	480 ml
1 teaspoon baking soda	5 ml
½ teaspoon baking powder	2 ml
¾ teaspoon cinnamon	4 ml
¼ teaspoon ground nutmeg	1 ml
¾ cup chopped pecans	180 ml

Topping:

½ cup chopped pecans	120 ml
½ teaspoon cinnamon	2 ml
½ cup packed brown sugar	120 ml

- Preheat oven to 350° (176° C).

- Combine sugar, applesauce, oil, eggs, milk and almond extract and mix well.

- Combine all dry ingredients and ¼ teaspoon (1 ml) salt, add to sugar mixture and mix well. Fold in pecans.

- Pour into 9 x 5-inch (23 x 13 cm) sprayed, floured loaf pan.

- For topping, combine pecans, cinnamon and brown sugar. Sprinkle over batter. Bake for 1 hour 5 minutes. Bread is done when toothpick inserted in center comes out clean. Cool on rack.

Banana-Pineapple Loaf

1 cup (2 sticks) butter, softened	240 ml
2 cups sugar	480 ml
4 eggs	
1 cup mashed ripe bananas	240 ml
3¾ cups flour	890 ml
2 teaspoons baking powder	10 ml
2 teaspoons baking soda	10 ml
1 (15 ounce) can crushed pineapple with juice	425 g
1 cup chopped pecans	240 ml

- Preheat oven to 325° (162° C). Cream butter and sugar, add eggs and beat until fluffy. Stir in bananas.

- Stir in dry ingredients and ½ teaspoon (2 ml) salt. (It will be stiff.) Fold in pineapple and pecans.

- Pour into 2 (9 x 5-inch/23 x 13 cm) sprayed, floured loaf pans and bake for 1 hour 10 minutes. Bread is done when toothpick inserted in center comes out clean. Cool several minutes before removing from pan.

Spicy Orange Butter:

1 cup (2 sticks) butter, softened	240 ml
1 cup powdered sugar	240 ml
2 teaspoons orange juice	10 ml
½ teaspoon nutmeg	2 ml
¾ teaspoon cinnamon	4 ml
½ teaspoon orange peel	2 ml
1½ teaspoons orange extract	7 ml

- Combine all ingredients and mix well. Make this spread and place in little half pint jars with lids and sell along with this bread. Chill until time to transport to bake sale.

Blueberry-Lemon Bread

1¾ cups flour	420 ml
1 teaspoon baking powder	5 ml
6 tablespoons (¾ stick) butter, softened	90 ml
1 cup sugar	240 ml
2 eggs	
2 teaspoons grated lemon peel	10 ml
½ cup milk	120 ml
1½ cups frozen blueberries, thawed, well drained	360 ml
½ cup sugar	120 ml
3 tablespoons lemon juice	45 ml

- Preheat oven to 350° (176° C). Combine flour, baking powder and ¼ teaspoon (1 ml) salt in small bowl and set aside.

- Use mixer to cream butter and sugar until light and fluffy. Add eggs, one at a time, and beat well after each addition. Add lemon peel and mix in dry ingredients, alternately with milk, beginning and ending with dry ingredients.

- Fold in blueberries. Spoon batter into 9 x 5-inch (23 x 13 cm) sprayed, floured loaf pan. Bake for 1 hour 5 minutes or until toothpick inserted in center comes out clean.

- Bring ½ cup (120 ml) sugar and lemon juice to boil in small saucepan and stir until sugar dissolves.

- While bread is still hot, pierce top several times with toothpick. Pour hot lemon mixture over loaf while still in pan. Cool 30 minutes on rack. Turn bread out of pan and cool completely on rack.

Buttersticks

These are like breadsticks without going to the trouble of using yeast. Good with pasta or salads too!

2 cups buttermilk baking mix	480 ml
1 tablespoon dried onion flakes	15 ml
1 egg	
⅓ - ½ cup milk	80 ml
½ cup (1 stick) butter	120 ml
2 tablespoons dried parsley flakes	30 ml
1½ teaspoons Italian herb seasoning	7 ml
½ teaspoon paprika	2 ml
⅓ cup grated parmesan cheese	80 ml

- Preheat oven to 375° (190° C).

- Combine baking mix, onion flakes, egg and just enough milk to make thick dough. Turn dough on lightly floured surface and knead lightly. On wax paper, pat into 9 x 13-inch (23 x 33 cm) rectangle shape.

- Add butter to 10 x 14-inch (25 x 36 cm) pan and melt in hot oven. Cut dough into 12 or 14 strips with sharp knife or pizza cutter. Cut each strip in half and place evenly on top of melted butter.

- Combine parsley flakes, Italian seasoning, paprika and parmesan cheese and sprinkle mixture over strips. Bake for 10 to 12 minutes or until golden brown. Serve hot.

TIP: Make note on label that these buttersticks are to be served hot by placing in a 300° (148° C) oven for about 10 minutes.

Poppy Seed Bread

3¾ cups biscuit mix	890 ml
1½ cups shredded cheddar cheese	360 ml
1 tablespoon poppy seeds	15 ml
1 egg, beaten	
1½ cups milk	360 ml

- Preheat oven to 350° (176° C).

- Combine all ingredients and beat vigorously for 1 minute. Pour into 9 x 5-inch (23 x 13 cm) sprayed, floured loaf pan.

- Bake for 50 to 60 minutes. Bread is done when toothpick inserted in center comes out clean. Remove from pan and cool before slicing.

Mincemeat Bread

1¾ cups flour	420 ml
1¼ cups sugar	300 ml
2½ teaspoons baking powder	12 ml
2 eggs, beaten	
1 teaspoon vanilla	5 ml
1½ cups prepared mincemeat	360 ml
¾ cup chopped pecans	180 ml
⅓ cup shortening, melted	80 ml

Glaze:

1 cup powdered sugar	240 ml
1 tablespoon milk	15 ml
¼ cup finely chopped pecans	60 ml

- Preheat oven to 350° (176° C).

- In large bowl combine flour, sugar, baking powder and ½ teaspoon (2 ml) salt.

- In medium bowl combine eggs, vanilla, mincemeat and pecans and mix well. Stir in melted shortening and mix quickly.

- Pour egg mixture into dry ingredients and stir only enough to moisten flour. Batter will be stiff. Spoon batter into 9 x 5-inch (23 x 13 cm) sprayed, floured pan.

- Bake for 1 hour or until toothpick inserted in center comes out clean. Cool 15 minutes, remove from pan and cool completely.

- Mix powdered sugar and milk and stir until smooth. Stir in pecans and spread over top of loaf.

Coconut Bread

1¼ cups shredded coconut	300 ml
2⅔ cups flour	640 ml
1¼ cups sugar	300 ml
4 teaspoons baking powder	20 ml
1½ cups milk	360 ml
1 egg	
2 tablespoons oil	30 ml
1¼ teaspoons coconut extract	6 ml

- Preheat oven to 300° (148° C). Toast coconut on ungreased baking sheet for 15 minutes; stir 2 times. Cool. Turn oven temperature up to 350° (176° C).

- Sift flour, sugar, baking powder and 1 teaspoon (5 ml) salt into mixing bowl and stir in coconut. In 2-cup (480 ml) measure combine milk, egg, oil and coconut extract. Beat until well blended.

- Add liquid mixture to dry ingredients all at once and mix lightly. Pour batter into 9 x 5-inch (23 x 13 cm) sprayed, floured loaf pan and bake for 1 hour 5 minutes. Bread is done when toothpick inserted in center comes out clean. Cool. Can be served with Strawberry Butter.

Strawberry Butter:

1¼ cups powdered sugar	300 ml
1 (10 ounce) package frozen strawberries,	
thawed, drained	280 g
1 cup (2 sticks) butter, softened	240 ml

- Place all ingredients in food processor and blend well. Chill.

Glazed Lemon Bread

¾ cup (1½ sticks) butter	180 ml
2 cups sugar	480 ml
4 eggs, slightly beaten	
½ teaspoon baking soda	2 ml
3 cups flour	710 ml
1 cup buttermilk	240 ml
2 tablespoons grated lemon rind	30 ml
1 cup chopped pecans	240 ml

Glaze:

Juice of 2 lemons	
1 cup powdered sugar	240 ml

- Preheat oven to 325° (162° C).

- Cream butter and sugar in large bowl and mix in eggs. Add dry ingredients and ½ teaspoon (2 ml) salt alternately with buttermilk and lemon rind. Stir in chopped pecans and pour into 9 x 5-inch (23 x 13 cm) sprayed, floured loaf pan. Bake for 40 minutes or until toothpick inserted in center comes out clean. Remove from oven and punch holes in bread with toothpick and pour glaze over bread while it is still hot. Cool completely.

BAKE SALE TIP:

Cut about 20 x 20-inch (50 x 50 cm) square of yellow plastic wrap, place loaf in center and pull up corners of plastic wrap and tie with a yellow ribbon and tag that says: Glazed Lemon Bread.

Island-Mango Bread

This is wonderful, moist and delicious!
It's great toasted for breakfast.

2 cups flour	480 ml
1 teaspoon baking soda	5 ml
1 teaspoon cinnamon	5 ml
1 cup sugar	240 ml
3 eggs, beaten	
¾ cup plus 1 tablespoon oil	180 ml/15 ml
2 cups peeled, seeded, finely diced mangoes	480 ml
1 teaspoon lemon juice	5 ml
⅓ cup shredded coconut	180 ml
⅔ cup chopped pecans	160 ml

- Preheat oven to 350° (176°).

- In large bowl, combine flour, baking soda, cinnamon, ¼ teaspoon (1 ml) salt and sugar and mix well.

- In separate bowl, stir eggs, oil, mangoes and lemon juice. Pour into flour mixture and mix well by hand.

- Stir in coconut and pecans and pour into 2 (8 x 4-inch/20 x 10 cm) sprayed, floured small loaf pans. Bake for 40 to 45 minutes. After 40 minutes insert toothpick in center. If it comes out clean, it is done.

TIP: To get 2 cups (480 ml) diced mangoes, you will need at least 2 ripe mangoes.

BAKE SALE TIP:

Write recipe on a recipe card and attach it to your packaging for the bake sale.

Strawberry Bread

3 cups flour	710 ml
2 cups sugar	480 ml
1 teaspoon baking soda	5 ml
2 teaspoons cinnamon	10 ml
3 large eggs, beaten	
1 cup oil	240 ml
1¼ cups chopped pecans	300 ml
2 (10 ounce) packages frozen sweetened	
strawberries with juice, thawed	2 (280 g)

- Preheat oven to 325° (162° C).

- Combine flour, sugar, 1 teaspoon (5 ml) salt, baking soda and cinnamon into large mixing bowl. Mix in eggs and oil. Fold in pecans and strawberries and mix well.

- Pour into 2 (9 x 5-inch/23 x 13 cm) sprayed, floured loaf pans and bake for 1 hour 10 minutes. Bread is done when toothpick inserted in center comes out clean. Cool several minutes before removing from pan.

Pineapple-Pecan Spread:

2 (8 ounce) packages cream cheese, softened	2 (227 g)
1 (8 ounce) can crushed pineapple with juice	227 g
¾ cup chopped pecans	180 ml

- In mixing bowl, beat cream cheese until smooth. Drain pineapple and save juice. Add crushed pineapple to cream cheese. Stir by hand and add just enough juice to make mixture spreadable. Add pecans and chill. Spread on slices of Strawberry Bread.

Sweet Apple Loaf

Toast this and serve it for breakfast or
spread cream cheese on it and have it for lunch. It's great.

⅔ cup (1⅓ sticks) butter	160 ml
2 cups sugar	480 ml
4 eggs	
2 cups applesauce	480 ml
⅓ cup milk	80 ml
1 tablespoon lemon juice	15 ml
4 cups flour	1 L
1 teaspoon cinnamon	5 ml
2 teaspoons baking powder	10 ml
1 teaspoon baking soda	5 ml
1½ cups chopped pecans	360 ml
¾ cup chopped maraschino cherries, well drained	180 ml

- Preheat oven to 325° (162° C).

- Cream butter, sugar and eggs and beat for several minutes. Stir in applesauce, milk and lemon juice.

- Sift flour, cinnamon, baking powder, baking soda and 1 teaspoon (5 ml) salt, add to first mixture and mix well. Fold in pecans and cherries.

- Pour into 3 (9 x 5-inch/23 x 13 cm) sprayed, floured loaf pans and bake for 1 hour. Bread is done when toothpick inserted in center comes out clean. Set aside for 10 to 15 minutes, remove from pans and cool on rack.

Yellow-Sweet Bread

1 (18 ounce) box yellow cake mix	510 g
1 (3.5 ounce) package instant vanilla pudding	100 g
¾ cup oil	180 ml
4 eggs	
1 teaspoon vanilla	5 ml
½ cup sugar	120 ml
2 teaspoons cinnamon	10 ml

Glaze:

1 cup powdered sugar	240 ml
2 tablespoons milk	30 ml
2 teaspoons vanilla	10 ml

- Preheat oven to 350° (176° C).

- In mixing bowl, beat cake mix, pudding, oil, eggs, vanilla and ¾ cup (180 ml) water. Pour half batter into 2 (9 x 5-inch/23 x 13 cm) sprayed, floured loaf pans.

- Combine sugar and cinnamon and sprinkle over batter. Run knife through to make ribbons of color. Spoon on remaining batter and bake for 40 minutes.

- For glaze, combine powdered sugar, milk and vanilla and mix well. While bread is still warm, spread glaze over top of each loaf.

Zucchini Bread

3 eggs
2 cups sugar   480 ml
1 cup oil   240 ml
3 teaspoons vanilla   15 ml
2 cups grated zucchini   480 ml
2 cups flour   480 ml
1 tablespoon cinnamon   15 ml
¼ teaspoon baking powder   1 ml
2 teaspoons baking soda   10 ml
1 cup chopped pecans   240 ml

- Preheat oven to 325° (162° C).

- Beat eggs until fluffy and add sugar, oil and vanilla. Beat until thick and lemon colored.

- Stir in zucchini, flour, cinnamon, baking powder, 1 teaspoon (5 ml) salt and baking soda. Fold in pecans and spoon into 2 (9 x 5-inch/23 x 13 cm) sprayed, floured loaf pans.

- Bake for 55 minutes. Cool in pan about 10 minutes before removing from loaf pan.

Pineapple-Cranberry Pull-Apart Rolls

1 (12 ounce) package frozen orange rolls, slightly thawed	340 g
1 (3.4 ounce) package cook-and-serve vanilla pudding	100 g
¼ cup finely chopped dried, sweetened pineapple	60 ml
¼ cup Craisins® (dried cranberries)	60 ml
½ cup (1 stick) butter, melted	120 ml

- Preheat oven to 350° (176° C).

- Cut rolls in half and roll in dry pudding mix and arrange, alternating with pineapple and cranberries in sprayed bundt pan.

- Sprinkle remaining pudding over rolls. Pour melted butter over top, cover with plastic wrap and let rise until double in size. Remove wrap and bake for 15 minutes.

- Remove from oven, cover with foil and bake additional 15 to 20 minutes. When done, immediately invert onto plastic serving platter. When cool, drizzle with frosting from rolls.

BAKE SALE TIP:

Place pieces of dried, sweetened pineapple around rolls for decoration. Cut 30-inch (77 cm) piece of plastic wrap and place serving platter in center. Pull up sides of plastic wrap about 10 inches (25 cm) and tie with colorful ribbon.

Christmas Morning Preserves

This is a delicacy ... a very special treat.

2 cups dried apricots	480 ml
2 cups chunk pineapple with juice	480 ml
2½ cups sugar	600 ml
3 tablespoons lemon juice	45 ml
1 (6 ounce) bottle red maraschino cherries	168 g
1 (6 ounce) bottle green maraschino cherries	168 g

- Wash apricots and simmer for 30 minutes in just enough water to cover apricots.

- Add pineapple, pineapple juice, sugar and lemon juice and cook slowly, stirring often, until thick and clear, about 40 minutes. Just before it is done, use potato masher to mash it up just a little.

- Drain cherries, cut in half and add to mixture. Heat again, pour into hot sterilized jars and seal.

- Process in boiling water bath for 20 minutes or keep in refrigerator as gift.

BAKE SALE TIP:

This would be good packaged with the Poppy Seed Bread or Mincemeat Bread. Place preserves in half pint jars with lids and sell with any one of our delicious breads.

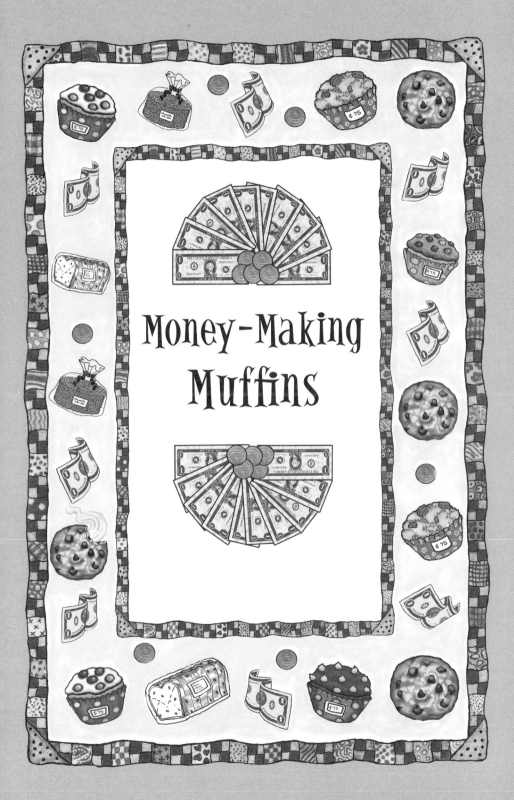

Money-Making Muffins

Apricot-Pineapple Muffins

This is a real winner ... a bestseller!

⅓ cup finely cut dried apricots	80 ml
½ cup (1 stick) butter, softened	120 ml
1 cup sugar	240 ml
1 egg	
1 (8 ounce) can crushed pineapple with juice	227 g
1¼ cups flour	300 ml
½ teaspoon baking soda	2 ml
½ cup quick-rolled oats	120 ml

- Preheat oven to 350° (176° C).

- Cut apricots with kitchen scissors and set aside. Use mixer to cream butter and sugar until smooth. Add egg and pineapple and beat well.

- Add all dry ingredients with ½ teaspoon (2 ml) salt and mix well. Fold in apricots.

- Spoon into 12 sprayed muffin pans or use paper liners and bake for 20 minutes.

Applesauce-Spice Muffins

1 cup (2 sticks) butter, softened	240 ml
1 cup packed brown sugar	240 ml
1 cup sugar	240 ml
2 eggs	
1¾ cups applesauce	420 ml
2 teaspoons cinnamon	10 ml
1 teaspoon allspice	5 ml
½ teaspoon ground cloves	2 ml
2 teaspoons baking soda	10 ml
3½ cups flour	830 ml
1½ cups chopped pecans	360 ml

- Preheat oven to 375° (190° C).

- Use mixer to cream butter and both sugars. Add eggs, applesauce, spices, ½ teaspoon (2 ml) salt, baking soda and flour and mix well. Add pecans and stir well.

- Pour into 28 sprayed muffin cups. Bake for 16 minutes.

Banana-Bran Muffins

1 cup bran flakes	240 ml
1 cup milk	240 ml
2 medium bananas, mashed	
⅓ cup oil	80 ml
1 cup flour	240 ml
4 teaspoons baking powder	20 ml
¼ teaspoon baking soda	1 ml
⅔ cup sugar	160 ml
1 egg	

- Preheat oven to 400° (204° C). In mixing bowl, combine bran flakes, milk, bananas and oil, mix and let stand for 5 minutes. Sift flour, baking powder, baking soda and ½ teaspoon (2 ml) salt and add to banana mixture. Add sugar, egg and mix only until all combine. Fill 12 large sprayed muffin cups and bake for 20 minutes.

Blue-Raspberry Muffins

1 (16 ounce) box blueberry muffin mix with blueberries	.5 kg
1 egg	
⅓ cup red raspberry jam	80 ml
¼ cup sliced almonds	60 ml

- Preheat oven to 375° (190° C). Rinse blueberries and drain. In bowl, combine muffin mix, egg and ½ cup (120 ml) water. Stir until moist and break up lumps in mix. Fill 8 paper-lined muffin cups half full of batter. Combine raspberry jam with blueberries. Spoon mixture on top of batter. Cover with remaining batter and sprinkle almonds over top. Bake for about 18 minutes or until light brown.

Double-Maple Muffins

1½ cups flour	360 ml
¼ cup sugar	60 ml
3 teaspoons baking powder	15 ml
½ teaspoon cinnamon	2 ml
¼ cup shortening	60 ml
¾ cup quick-cooking oats	180 ml
1 egg, beaten	
½ cup milk	120 ml
½ cup maple syrup	120 ml

- Preheat oven to 400° (204° C).

- Sift flour, sugar, baking powder, ½ teaspoon (2 ml) salt and cinnamon. Cut in shortening until mixture resembles coarse crumbs.

- Stir in oats, egg, milk and syrup and stir only until dry ingredients are moist. Fill 12 sprayed muffin cups two-thirds full and bake for 18 to 20 minutes. Let stand a few minutes before removing from pan.

Glaze:

1 tablespoon butter, softened	15 ml
2 tablespoons maple syrup	30 ml
⅓ cup powdered sugar	80 ml

- Combine butter, maple syrup and powdered sugar and beat thoroughly. Drizzle over hot muffins.

Ginger Muffins

¾ cup (1½ sticks) butter, softened	180 ml
¾ cup sugar	180 ml
¼ cup corn syrup	60 ml
¼ cup sorghum molasses	60 ml
2 eggs	
1 teaspoon baking soda	5 ml
½ cup buttermilk*	120 ml
2 cups flour	480 ml
1 teaspoon ground ginger	5 ml
¼ teaspoon cinnamon	1 ml
½ cup chopped pecans	120 ml

- Preheat oven to 350° (176° C).

- In mixing bowl, combine butter, sugar, syrup and molasses and mix well. Add eggs and beat well.

- Stir baking soda into buttermilk, add to butter-sugar mixture and beat. Add flour, pinch of salt, ginger and cinnamon and beat. Stir in pecans and mix well.

- Pour into 20 to 24 sprayed muffin cups and bake for 16 to 18 minutes.

    TIP: To make buttermilk, mix 1 cup (240 ml) milk with 1 tablespoon (15 ml) lemon juice or vinegar and let milk rest about 10 minutes.

Hidden Secret Muffins

Filling:

1 (8 ounce) package cream cheese, softened	227 g
1 egg	
⅓ cup sugar	80 ml
1 tablespoon grated orange rind	15 ml

Muffins:

1 cup (2 sticks) butter, softened	240 ml
1¾ cups sugar	420 ml
3 eggs	
3 cups flour	710 ml
2 teaspoons baking powder	10 ml
1 cup milk	240 ml
1 teaspoon almond extract	5 ml
1 cup slivered almonds	240 ml

- Preheat oven to 375° (190° C).

- To prepare filling, beat cream cheese, egg, sugar and orange rind and set aside.

- To prepare batter, cream butter and sugar until light and fluffy. Add eggs one at a time and beat after each addition.

- Mix flour and baking powder and add alternately with milk to butter-sugar mixture. Begin and end with flour. Add almond extract and fold in almonds.

- Fill 26 sprayed, floured muffin cups half full of batter. Spoon 1 heaping tablespoon (15 ml) filling in each muffin cup and top with remaining batter. Bake muffins for 20 to 25 minutes or until muffin bounces back when pressed or until they are light brown.

Maple-Spice Muffins

1¼ cups flour	300 ml
1½ cups whole wheat flour	360 ml
½ cup quick-cooking oats	120 ml
1 teaspoon baking soda	5 ml
2 teaspoons baking powder	10 ml
2 teaspoons cinnamon	10 ml
½ teaspoon ground cloves	2 ml
2 eggs	
1 (8 ounce) carton sour cream	227 g
1 cup maple syrup	240 ml
1 cup packed brown sugar	240 ml
½ cup oil	120 ml
1 banana, peeled, mashed	
1 cup chopped walnuts	240 ml

- Preheat oven to 375° (190° C).

- In mixing bowl, combine both flours, oats, baking soda, baking powder, cinnamon and cloves and mix. Add eggs, sour cream, maple syrup, brown sugar, oil and mashed banana. Stir well by hand.

- Add walnuts and pour into 24 paper lined muffin cups. Bake for 18 to 20 minutes.

Moist Pumpkin Muffins

1 (15 ounce) can pumpkin	425 g
3 eggs, slightly beaten	
½ cup oil	120 ml
1½ teaspoons ground cinnamon	7 ml
1 teaspoon baking soda	5 ml
1 (18 ounce) butter pecan cake mix	510 g
1 (16 ounce) can butter-cream icing	.5 kg

- Preheat oven to 350° (176° C).

- Combine pumpkin, eggs, oil, cinnamon and baking soda in mixing bowl and mix well. Add cake mix and beat 1 minute on low speed, then beat on high speed for 2 minutes.

- Fill paper-lined muffin cups two-thirds full and bake for 15 to 17 minutes or until toothpick inserted in center comes out clean. Cool and remove muffins from pan. Ice with butter-cream icing.

BAKE SALE TIP:

Place iced muffins on round plastic tray. Cut 30-inch (70 cm) piece of clear plastic wrap and place tray in center. Pull all edges of plastic wrap up about 10 inches (25 cm) and tie with colorful ribbon.

Harvest-Filled Muffins

1 (8 ounce) package cream cheese, softened	227 g
3 eggs, divided	
2½ cups sugar, divided	600 ml
2½ cups flour, divided	600 ml
⅓ cup chopped pecans	80 ml
3 tablespoons butter, melted	45 ml
2½ teaspoons cinnamon, divided	12 ml
2 teaspoons baking powder	10 ml
¼ teaspoon baking soda	1 ml
1¼ cups pumpkin	300 ml
⅓ cup oil	80 ml
½ teaspoon vanilla	2 ml

- Preheat oven to 375° (190° C).

- Beat cream cheese, 1 egg and 3 tablespoons (45 ml) sugar and set aside. Toss 5 tablespoons (75 ml) sugar, ½ cup (120 ml) flour, pecans, butter and ½ teaspoon (2 ml) cinnamon and set aside.

- Combine remaining sugar, remaining flour, ½ teaspoon (2 ml) salt, baking powder, baking soda and remaining cinnamon.

- Lightly beat remaining 2 eggs, pumpkin, oil and vanilla. Pour pumpkin mixture into flour mixture and mix with fork until moist.

- Spray 24 muffin cups and divide half batter evenly among muffin cups. Place 2 teaspoonfuls (10 ml) cream cheese mixture in center of each cup and fill with remaining batter. Sprinkle pecan mixture over top of each muffin and bake for 20 to 25 minutes or until toothpick inserted into center comes out clean.

Pass the
Coffee Cakes

Cherry-Nut Breakfast Cake

1 (8 ounce) package cream cheese, softened	227 g
1 cup (2 sticks) butter, softened	240 ml
1½ cups sugar	360 ml
1½ teaspoons vanilla	7 ml
3 eggs	
2¼ cups flour	540 ml
1½ teaspoons baking powder	7 ml
1 (10 ounce) jar maraschino cherries, drained	280 g
½ cup chopped pecans	120 ml

Glaze:

1½ cups powdered sugar	360 ml
2½ tablespoons milk	35 ml
2 tablespoons (¼ stick) butter, melted	30 ml
½ teaspoon almond extract	2 ml
½ cup chopped pecans	120 ml

- Preheat oven to 350° (176° C).

- In large mixing bowl, blend cream cheese, butter, sugar, vanilla and eggs and beat for 3 minutes. Add flour and baking powder and beat well.

- Cut each cherry into 3 or 4 pieces; then fold in cherries and pecans. Pour batter into 9 x 13-inch (23 x 33 cm) sprayed, floured baking pan and bake for 40 minutes.

- Just before cake is done, combine powdered sugar, milk, butter and almond extract. Pour glaze over cake while it is still warm and top with pecans.

Cranberry-Almond Cake

This is good for dessert or as a coffee cake for breakfast.

½ cup (1 stick) butter, softened	120 ml
1 cup sugar	240 ml
2 eggs	
1 teaspoon almond extract	5 ml
2 cups flour	480 ml
1 teaspoon baking powder	5 ml
1 (8 ounce) carton sour cream	227 g
1 cup whole cranberry sauce	240 ml
¾ cup chopped slivered almonds	180 ml

Glaze:

1½ cups powdered sugar	360 ml
3 tablespoons milk	45 ml
½ teaspoon almond extract	2 ml

- Preheat oven to 350° (176° C).

- Cream butter and sugar and beat until fluffy.

- Add eggs one at a time, beating after each addition, and add almond extract.

- Combine flour, baking powder and ¼ teaspoon (1 ml) salt. Add flour mixture and sour cream, alternately to sugar mixture, beginning and ending with flour mixture.

- Fold in cranberry sauce and almonds. Pour batter into 9 x 13-inch (23 x 33 cm) sprayed, floured baking pan.

- Bake for 30 to 35 minutes or until toothpick inserted in center comes out clean.

- Combine glaze ingredients and drizzle over warm cake.

French-Apple Coffee Cake

*This is an excellent cake to have on hand
for Sunday morning or when you have company.*

¾ cup sugar	180 ml
1 cup packed light brown sugar	240 ml
⅔ cup buttermilk	160 ml
2 eggs	
2½ cups flour	600 ml
2 teaspoons baking soda	10 ml
2 teaspoons cinnamon	10 ml
¼ cup white raisins	60 ml
1 (20 ounce) can apple pie filling, apples cut up	567 g
½ cup (1 stick) butter, melted	120 ml

Topping:

1 teaspoon cinnamon	5 ml
⅔ cup packed light brown sugar	160 ml
⅔ cup chopped walnuts	160 ml

- Preheat oven to 350° (176° C).

- In large bowl, mix both sugars, buttermilk and eggs. Add flour, baking soda, cinnamon and ½ teaspoon (2 ml) salt and mix well. Fold in raisins and pie filling. (Apples can be cut up by placing pie filling on plate and cut into smaller pieces.)

- Spread into 9 x 13-inch (23 x 33 cm) sprayed, floured baking pan.

- Combine all topping ingredients and sprinkle over top of cake. Bake for 45 minutes.

- When cake is done, drizzle melted butter over top of cake.

Good Glory Coffee Cake

2⅓ cups flour	560 ml
1½ cups sugar	360 ml
¾ cup shortening	180 ml
2 teaspoons baking powder	10 ml
¾ cup milk	180 ml
2 eggs	
1 teaspoon vanilla	5 ml
1 (3 ounce) package cream cheese, softened	84 g
1 (14 ounce) can sweetened condensed milk	396 g
⅓ cup lemon juice	80 ml
1 (20 ounce) can peach pie filling	567 g
2 teaspoons cinnamon	10 ml
¾ cup chopped pecans	180 ml

- Preheat oven to 350° (176° C).

- In mixing bowl, combine flour, sugar and ¾ teaspoon (4 ml) salt. Cut in shortening until crumbly. Set aside 1 cup (240 ml) crumb mixture.

- To remaining crumb mixture, add baking powder, milk, eggs and vanilla. Beat on medium speed for 2 minutes.

- Spread in 9 x 13-inch (23 x 33 cm) sprayed, floured baking pan. Bake for 25 minutes.

- In another bowl, beat cream cheese and sweetened condensed milk until fluffy. Cut each peach in pie filling into 3 pieces and add to cream cheese mixture. Gradually fold in lemon juice, peach pie filling and cinnamon. Spoon this mixture over hot cake. Add pecans to remaining crumb mixture and sprinkle on top of cake. Bake another 25 minutes.

Mincemeat-Crumb Coffee Cake

Topping:

2 tablespoons flour	30 ml
1/3 cup sugar	80 ml
1 1/2 teaspoons cinnamon	7 ml
2 tablespoons butter	30 ml

Cake:

1 1/2 cups flour	360 ml
3/4 cup sugar	180 ml
2 teaspoons baking powder	10 ml
1 egg	
1/2 cup milk	120 ml
3 tablespoons butter, melted, cooled	45 ml
1 cup prepared mincemeat	240 ml
1/2 cup chopped pecans	120 ml

- Preheat oven to 375° (190° C).

- For topping, mix dry ingredients, cut in butter until mixture becomes crumbly and set aside.

- In mixing bowl, mix flour, sugar, baking powder and 1/2 teaspoon (2 ml) salt.

- Beat egg with milk and melted butter. Add egg mixture to flour mixture and stir until smooth. Stir in mincemeat and pecans.

- Spread batter into 10-inch (25 cm) sprayed, floured deep-dish pie plate and sprinkle with topping.

- Bake for about 40 minutes or until toothpick inserted in center comes out clean.

Moist Toffee Coffee Cake

¼ cup instant coffee granules	60 ml
⅓ cup oil	80 ml
3 eggs, slightly beaten	
1 (18 ounce) box yellow cake mix	510 g
½ cup chopped pecans	120 ml
1 (7.5 ounce) package Bits O'Brickle®, divided	210 g
1 (16 ounce) carton caramel icing	.5 kg

- Preheat oven to 350° (176° C).

- In small cup, dissolve coffee granules in ¼ cup (60 ml) boiling water. Combine 1 cup (240 ml) water, oil, eggs and coffee mixture in large bowl and slowly add cake mix while beating with mixer. Increase speed to medium, beat 2 minutes and scrape bowl occasionally.

- Stir in pecans and half Brickle chips. Pour into 9 x 13-inch (23 x 33 cm) sprayed, floured foil baking pan. Place on cookie sheet before placing in oven and bake for 30 to 33 minutes or until toothpick inserted in center comes out clean. Cool at least 1 hour.

- Spread with caramel icing and sprinkle remaining package of Brickle chips on top.

BAKE SALE TIP:

This cake can be served for breakfast or dinner. Cover with plastic wrap and tightly secure on bottom. Just be sure to transport cake on level cookie sheet so icing will remain firm and not crack.

Quick Coffee Cake

¼ cup (½ stick) butter, softened	60 ml
½ cup sugar	120 ml
2 eggs, beaten	
1½ cups flour	360 ml
2 teaspoons baking powder	10 ml
1 cup milk	240 ml
½ cup packed brown sugar	120 ml
¾ cup chopped pecans	180 ml
1 teaspoon cinnamon	5 ml
¼ teaspoon nutmeg	1 ml
1 tablespoon butter, melted	15 ml
1 tablespoon flour	15 ml

- Preheat oven to 350° (176° C).

- In large bowl, cream butter and sugar and stir in beaten eggs. Add flour and baking powder alternately with milk. Spoon half of dough into 8 x 8-inch (20 x 20 cm) sprayed foil pan.

- Combine brown sugar, pecans, cinnamon, nutmeg, butter and 1 tablespoon (15 ml) flour and mix well. Sprinkle half this mixture over batter and spoon on remaining dough. Cover with remaining sugar-pecan mixture and bake for 30 minutes.

   TIP: With coffee cake made in foil pan, it can be heated up the next morning for a quick breakfast.

Cranberry-Coffee Cake

2 eggs
1 cup mayonnaise   240 ml
1 (18 ounce) box spice cake mix   510 g
1 (16 ounce) can whole cranberry sauce   .5 kg
Powdered sugar

- Preheat oven to 325° (162° C).

- Beat eggs, mayonnaise and cake mix with mixer and fold in cranberry sauce.

- Pour into 9 x 13-inch (23 x 33 cm) sprayed, floured baking pan.

- Bake for 45 minutes. Cake is done when toothpick inserted in center comes out clean.

- After cake cools, dust with powdered sugar using a flour sifter.

  TIP: If you would rather have an icing on this coffee cake, use 1 (16 ounce/.5 kg) can creamy vanilla icing.

Breakfast Cinnamon Cake

⅔ cup packed brown sugar	160 ml
1 tablespoon grated orange peel	15 ml
2 (12.4 ounce each) refrigerated	
cinnamon rolls	2 (340 g)

- Preheat oven to 375° (190° C).

- Coat 10-inch (25 cm) bundt pan with cooking spray. In small bowl, combine brown sugar and orange peel.

- Open cans of rolls (save icing) and cut each in quarters. Coat each quarter with cooking spray. Dip in sugar-orange mixture and arrange evenly in bundt pan; gently press down. Bake 30 minutes until light brown and about double in size. Cool slightly in pan.

- Invert serving plate on top of pan and with oven mitts, hold plate and pan together and invert. Remove pan. Spread icing unevenly over top of cake and serve warm.

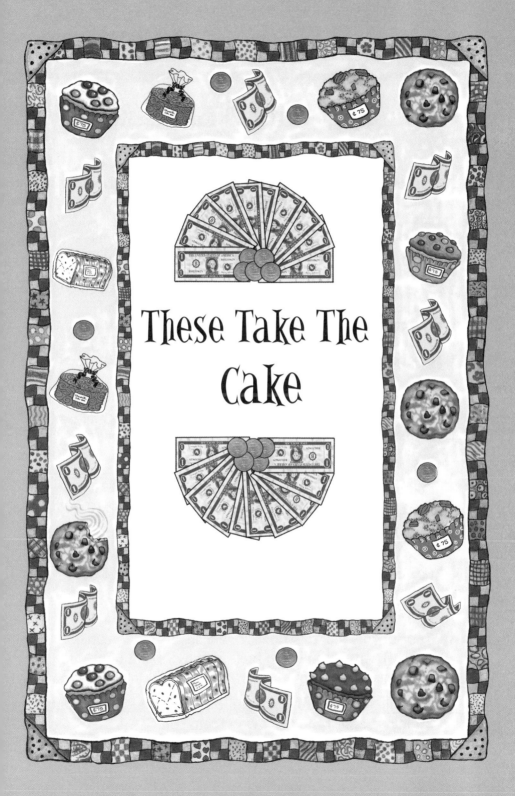

Apple-Date Pecan Cake

This cake is so moist and full of goodies!

2 cups sugar	480 ml
1½ cups oil	360 ml
3 eggs	
2 teaspoons vanilla	10 ml
2½ cups flour	600 ml
1 teaspoon baking soda	5 ml
1½ teaspoons cinnamon	7 ml
¼ teaspoon ground ginger	1 ml
3 cups chopped apples	710 ml
1 (8 ounce) package pitted chopped dates	227 g
1 cup chopped pecans	240 ml

Glaze:

1 cup sugar	240 ml
1 teaspoon almond extract	5 ml

- Preheat oven to 325° (162° C).

- Combine sugar, oil, eggs and vanilla in mixing bowl and beat well. Add flour, baking soda, ½ teaspoon (2 ml) salt, cinnamon and ginger and beat well.

- Fold in apples, dates and pecans and pour into 10-inch (25 cm) sprayed, floured tube pan. Bake for 1 hour 20 minutes or until toothpick inserted in center comes out clean.

- Just before cake is done, bring sugar and ⅓ cup (80 ml) water to rolling boil. Remove from heat and add almond extract.

- Pour glaze over hot cake while still in pan. Cool about 20 minutes before removing from pan.

Apple-Walnut Cake

2 cups sugar	480 ml
3 cups flour	710 ml
1 teaspoon baking soda	5 ml
1 teaspoon cinnamon	5 ml
1½ cups oil	360 ml
3 large eggs, slightly beaten	
1 teaspoon vanilla	5 ml
3 cups peeled, chopped baking apples	710 ml
1½ cups chopped walnuts	360 ml
Marshmallow Heaven Icing	

- Preheat oven to 350° (176° C).

- Spray 10-cup (2.5 L) tube pan. Mix sugar, flour, baking soda, cinnamon and 1 teaspoon (5 ml) salt in large bowl and mix until they blend well.

- Stir in oil, eggs and vanilla and mix well. Fold in chopped apples and walnuts and spoon into pan.

- Bake for 1 hour or until toothpick inserted in center comes out clean. Cool in pan 10 minutes before inverting onto rack to cool completely.

- Ice cake with Marshmallow Heaven Icing on page 101.

Old-Fashioned Applesauce-Spice Cake

1 (18 ounce) box spice cake mix	510 g
3 eggs	
1¼ cup applesauce	300 ml
⅓ cup oil	80 ml
1 cup chopped pecans	240 ml

Frosting:

1 (8 ounce) can crushed pineapple with juice	227 g
½ cup (1 stick) butter	120 ml
1 (16 ounce) box powdered sugar	.5 kg
1 cup flaked coconut	240 ml

- Preheat oven to 350° (176° C).

- With mixer, combine cake mix, eggs, applesauce and oil and beat on medium speed for 2 minutes. Stir in pecans and pour into 9 x 13-inch (23 x 33 cm) sprayed, floured foil baking pan. Bake for 40 minutes or until toothpick inserted in center comes out clean.

- In saucepan on high heat, combine pineapple and butter and boil 2 minutes. Remove from heat and stir in powdered sugar and coconut and mix well. Pour over hot cake.

Easy Applesauce-Spice Cake

1 (18 ounce) box spice cake mix	510 g
3 eggs	
1¼ cups applesauce	300 ml
⅓ cup oil	80 ml
1 cup chopped walnuts	240 ml

Icing:

1 (16 ounce) can vanilla icing	.5 kg
½ teaspoon cinnamon	2 ml

- Preheat oven to 350° (176° C).

- Beat cake mix, eggs, applesauce and oil with mixer on medium speed for 2 minutes. Stir in walnuts.

- Pour into 9 x 13-inch (23 x 33 cm) sprayed, floured baking pan.

- Bake for 40 minutes. Cake is done when toothpick inserted in center comes out clean. Cool completely.

- Combine icing and cinnamon and spread over cake.

Best Fresh Apple Cake

1½ cups oil	360 ml
2 cups sugar	480 ml
3 eggs	
2½ cups sifted flour	600 ml
1 teaspoon baking soda	5 ml
2 teaspoons baking powder	10 ml
½ teaspoon cinnamon	2 ml
1 teaspoon vanilla	5 ml
3 cups peeled, grated apples	710 ml
1 cup chopped pecans	240 ml

Glaze:

2 tablespoons (¼ stick) butter, melted	30 ml
2 tablespoons milk	30 ml
1 cup powdered sugar	240 ml
1 teaspoon vanilla	5 ml
¼ teaspoon lemon extract	1 ml

- Preheat oven to 350° (176° C).

- In mixing bowl, combine oil, sugar and eggs and beat well.

- In separate bowl, sift flour, ½ teaspoon (2 ml) salt, baking soda, baking powder and cinnamon. Gradually add dry mixture to cream mixture.

- Add vanilla and fold in apples and pecans. Pour into sprayed tube pan. Bake for 1 hour.

- Remove from oven, cool and invert onto serving plate.

- Combine and mix all glaze ingredients and drizzle over cake.

Apricot-Brandy Cake

1 (18 ounce) box yellow cake mix	510 g
1 (3.4 ounce) package French vanilla pudding mix	100 g
4 eggs, slightly beaten	
1 (8 ounce) carton sour cream	227 g
½ teaspoon lemon extract	2 ml
½ cup brandy	120 ml
1 (15 ounce) can apricot halves with juice, quartered	425 g
1 cup powdered sugar	240 ml
1 tablespoon butter, melted	15 ml

- Preheat oven to 350° (176° C).

- Combine cake mix, pudding mix, eggs, sour cream, lemon extract and brandy in mixing bowl. Beat on medium speed 2 to 3 minutes and fold in drained apricots.

- Pour into sprayed, floured decorative bundt pan. Bake for 50 minutes or until toothpick inserted in thickest part comes out clean. Let cake cool 10 minutes and turn out on serving platter.

- Combine powdered sugar and melted butter with just enough apricot juice to make glaze spreadable. Let some glaze run down sides of cake.

Apricot-Pecan Cake

1 (18 ounce) box butter pecan cake mix	510 g
¼ cup oil	60 ml
3 eggs, slightly beaten	
1 (15 ounce) can apricot halves, drained, chopped	425 g
¾ cup chopped pecans	180 ml
1 cup apricot preserves	240 ml
1 (16 ounce) carton butter-cream icing	.5 kg
⅔ cup peach gummy candy rings	160 ml

- Preheat oven to 350° (176° C).

- Combine cake mix, 1 cup (240 ml) water, oil, eggs and chopped apricots in mixing bowl. Beat on low speed for 30 seconds, increase speed to medium and beat for 2 minutes.

- Stir in pecans and pour into 9 x 13-inch (23 x 13 cm) sprayed, floured foil pan.

- Bake for 40 to 45 minutes or until toothpick inserted in center comes out clean. Cool completely. Place apricot preserves in saucepan, heat on low until able to stir and remove from heat.

- Spread preserves over top of cake and spread icing over top of preserves.

BAKE SALE TIP:

Place iced muffins on round plastic tray. Cut 30-inch (70 cm) piece of clear plastic wrap and place tray in center. Pull all edges of plastic wrap up about 10 inches (25 cm) and tie with colorful ribbon.

Banana-Butter Cake

1 (18 ounce) box yellow cake mix	510 g
⅔ cup milk	160 ml
2 tablespoons oil	30 ml
1 egg	
2 ripe bananas	
3 (2 ounce) Butterfinger® candy bars, chopped, divided	3 (57 g)
½ cup chopped pecans	120 ml
1 (16 ounce) can white frosting	.5 kg

- Preheat over to 350° (176° C).

- Prepare cake batter according to package directions using milk, oil and egg.

- Mash bananas and stir into batter. Fold in about ¾ cup (180 ml) chopped Butterfinger® and chopped pecans.

- Pour into 9 x 13-inch (23 x 33 cm) sprayed, floured foil baking pan.

- Bake for 40 to 50 minutes or until toothpick inserted in center comes out clean.

- Cool and spread with frosting. Sprinkle remaining chopped Butterfinger® over top.

Coconut-Pecan Cake

Cake:

2 cups flour	480 ml
1½ cups sugar	360 ml
2 teaspoons baking soda	10 ml
1 (20 ounce) can crushed pineapple with juice	567 g

Icing:

1½ cups sugar	360 ml
1 (5 ounce) can evaporated milk	143 g
½ cup (1 stick) butter	120 ml
1 cup flaked coconut	240 ml
1 cup chopped pecans	240 ml
1 teaspoon vanilla	5 ml

- Preheat oven to 350° (176° C).

- Combine cake ingredients plus dash of salt with spoon and pour into 9 x 13-inch (23 x 33 cm) sprayed, floured baking pan. Bake for 35 minutes and leave in pan.

- Start icing just before cake is done. Combine sugar, milk and butter in saucepan. Boil for 2 minutes and stir constantly. Add coconut, pecans, vanilla and dash of salt and pour mixture over cake as soon as it comes out of oven.

- When cake is cool, cover with foil. Cut into squares before serving.

Delightful Pear Cake

This is a delightfully moist cake!

1 (15 ounce) can pears in light syrup with juice	425 g
1 (18 ounce) box white cake mix	510 g
2 egg whites	
1 egg	
Powdered sugar	

- Preheat oven to 350° (176° C).

- Drain pears, save liquid and chop pears.

- Place pears and liquid in mixing bowl and add cake mix, egg whites and egg. Beat on low speed for 30 seconds. Beat on high for 4 minutes.

- Pour batter into 10-inch (25 cm) sprayed, floured bundt pan.

- Bake for 50 to 55 minutes. Bake until toothpick inserted in center comes out clean. Cool in pan for 10 minutes. Cool completely and sprinkle powdered sugar over cake.

BAKE SALE TIP:

Let cake cool several hours before wrapping with plastic wrap.

Dirt-And-Worms Cake

This fun dessert is easy to make and children love it!
This is one mud cake you won't mind them eating! Also, it's fun
to put a plastic, toy trowel with it for the "gardener" to use.

1 (18 ounce) chocolate cake mix	510 g
⅓ cup oil	80 ml
3 eggs	
½ cup chocolate syrup	120 ml
1 (3 ounce) package instant chocolate fudge	
pudding mix	84 g
1¾ cups milk	420 ml
1 cup crushed chocolate graham crackers or	
other chocolate cookies	240 ml
7 candy gummy worms	

- Preheat oven to 350° (176° C).

- Prepare cake mix for 9 x 13-inch (23 x 33 cm) baking dish according to package directions using oil, eggs and 1¼ cups (300 ml) water and bake for 30 to 35 minutes.

- While cake is still hot, poke holes over entire surface with knife. Pour chocolate syrup evenly over cake, cool.

- In small bowl, beat pudding mix and milk for 2 minutes and set aside for 3 to 5 minutes. Smooth evenly over cake.

- Sprinkle half graham cracker crumbs over pudding. Score top of cake as you would slice into servings. No need to cut through to bottom. Push 1 end of each worm gently into crumb mixture and cover lightly with remaining crumbs. (Worms should appear to be poking out of the ground.) Chill until ready to serve.

Easy Breezy Favorite Cake

1 (18 ounce) butter-pecan cake mix	510 g
½ cup (1 stick) butter, softened	120 ml
3 eggs	
1 cup almond-toffee bits	240 ml
1 cup chopped pecans	240 ml
Powdered sugar	

- Preheat oven to 350° (176° C).

- Prepare cake mix according to package directions using butter, egg and 1¼ cups (300 ml) water. Fold in almond-toffee bits and pecans.

- Pour into sprayed, floured bundt cake pan.

- Bake for 45 minutes or until toothpick inserted in center comes out clean.

- Allow cake to cool 15 minutes and remove from pan. Dust with sifted powdered sugar.

Easy Pineapple Cake

2 cups sugar	480 ml
2 cups flour	480 ml
1 (20 ounce) can crushed pineapple with juice	567 g
1 teaspoon baking soda	5 ml

- Preheat oven to 350° (176° C).

- Combine all cake ingredients and mix by hand.

- Pour into 9 x 13-inch (23 x 33 cm) sprayed, floured baking pan.

- Bake for 30 to 35 minutes.

Icing:

1 (8 ounce) package cream cheese, softened	227 g
½ cup (1 stick) butter, melted	120 ml
1 cup powdered sugar	240 ml
1 cup chopped pecans	240 ml

- Combine cream cheese, butter and powdered sugar and beat with mixer.

- Add chopped pecans and spread over hot cake.

    TIP: This is no misprint; this recipe uses no eggs.

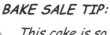

BAKE SALE TIP:

This cake is so easy you will want to bake 2 of them. Cut 1 in small squares and pass out to your buyers with a typed copy of this recipe as a way of saying, 'thank you' for visiting the bake sale.

French Vanilla Cake

1 (18 ounce) box French vanilla cake mix	510 g
1 pint vanilla ice cream, melted	.5 kg
3 eggs, beaten	
1 teaspoon vanilla extract	5 ml

- Preheat oven to 350° (176° C).

- In mixing bowl, beat all cake ingredients for 3 minutes on medium speed. Spoon into 10-inch (25 cm) sprayed, floured tube pan.

- Bake for 35 to 40 minutes or until toothpick inserted in center comes out clean. Cool in pan for about 20 minutes and invert onto cake plate. Cool completely before frosting.

Frosting:

1 (8 ounce) package cream cheese, softened	227 g
¼ cup (½ stick) butter, softened	60 ml
2 tablespoons coffee liqueur	30 ml
1½ cups powdered sugar	360 ml

- In mixing bowl, beat cream cheese, butter and liqueur on low speed until light and creamy. Gradually add powdered sugar and beat for about 2 minutes. Spread frosting on top and sides of cool cake.

  TIP: If you don't have coffee liqueur on hand, use 2 tablespoons (30 ml) brewed coffee with 1 teaspoon (5 ml) sugar.

Fruit Cocktail Cake

1½ cups sugar	360 ml
2 cups flour	480 ml
2 teaspoons baking soda	10 ml
2 eggs, beaten	
1 (15 ounce) can fruit cocktail with liquid	425 g
1 teaspoon vanilla	5 ml
1 teaspoon butter flavoring	5 ml
1 cup chopped pecans	240 ml
½ cup packed brown sugar	120 ml

Icing:

½ cup (1 stick) butter	120 ml
¾ cup sugar	180 ml
¾ cup packed brown sugar	180 ml
½ cup milk	120 ml
1 teaspoon vanilla	5 ml

- Preheat oven to 350° (176° C).

- In large bowl, combine sugar, flour, baking soda, eggs, fruit cocktail, vanilla and butter flavoring and mix well by hand. Pour batter in 9 x 13-inch (23 x 33 cm) foil baking pan.

- Combine pecans and ½ cup (120 ml) brown sugar and sprinkle over batter and bake for 30 minutes.

- Combine butter, both sugars and milk, bring to a boil and stir constantly. Cook 2 minutes, remove from heat and add vanilla. Pour over cake while both are still hot. Cool completely.

Glazed Gingerbread Cake

3 cups flour	710 ml
1½ teaspoons cinnamon	7 ml
1½ teaspoons ginger	7 ml
1 teaspoon baking powder	5 ml
1 teaspoon baking soda	5 ml
1 cup shortening	240 ml
¾ cup packed brown sugar	180 ml
2 eggs, slightly beaten	
1 cup light molasses	240 ml

Icing:

1 cup powdered sugar	240 ml
¼ teaspoon vanilla	1 ml
1 tablespoon lemon juice, more if needed	15 ml

- Preheat oven to 350° (176° C).

- Combine flour, cinnamon, ginger, baking powder and baking soda and set aside. Place shortening in mixing bowl and beat for 30 seconds.

- Add brown sugar and beat until fluffy. Add eggs and molasses and beat 1 minute. Stir in flour mixture and 1 cup (240 ml) water alternately to sugar-egg mixture and beat on low speed after each addition. Pour into 10-inch (25 cm) sprayed, floured bundt pan.

- Bake for 50 to 55 minutes or until toothpick inserted in center comes out clean. Cool in pan for 30 minutes then remove from pan. Cool completely.

- Combine powdered sugar, vanilla and 1 tablespoon (15 ml) lemon juice or more to reach drizzling consistency. Drizzle icing over top and down sides.

Hawaiian-Dream Cake

1 (18 ounce) box yellow cake mix	510 g
4 eggs	
¾ cup oil	180 ml
1 (20 ounce) can crushed pineapple with juice, divided	567 g
½ (7 ounce) package Smoothie Mix Skittles®	½ (198 g)

Icing:

½ cup (1 stick) butter	120 ml
1 (16 ounce) box powdered sugar	.5 kg
1 (6 ounce) can flaked coconut	168 g

- Preheat oven to 350° (176° C).

- In mixing bowl, combine cake mix, eggs, ½ pineapple and ½ juice and beat 4 minutes.

- Pour into 9 x 13-inch (23 x 33 cm) sprayed, floured foil baking pan.

- Bake for 30 to 35 minutes or until toothpick inserted in center comes out clean. Cool completely.

- Pour remaining pineapple juice and butter in medium saucepan and boil for 2 minutes.

- Add powdered sugar and coconut and mix well.

- Pierce holes in cake with knife. Pour hot icing over cake. After cakes cools, sprinkle or place Skittles® on top with plastic cover.

BAKE SALE TIP:

Bake and sell this delicious cake in a 9 x 13-inch (23 x 33 cm) foil baking pan.

Holiday Lemon-Pecan Cake

This is truly a holiday cake. It has the consistency of a fruitcake, but only pineapple and cherries for the fruit.

1 (1.5 ounce) bottle lemon extract	45 g
4 cups pecan halves	1 L
2 cups (4 sticks) butter	480 ml
3 cups sugar	710 ml
3½ cups flour, divided	830 ml
1½ teaspoons baking powder	7 ml
6 eggs, divided	
½ pound candied green pineapple, chopped	227 g
½ pound candied red cherries, halved	227 g
½ cup flour	120 ml

• Preheat oven to 275° (135° C).

• Pour lemon extract over pecans in medium bowl, toss and set aside. In large mixing bowl, cream butter and sugar until fluffy. Sift 3 cups (710 ml) flour and baking powder in separate bowl. Add eggs to butter-sugar mixture, 1 at a time, alternately with flour mixture.

• Add ½ cup (120 ml) flour to pineapple and cherries and mix so that flour covers fruit. Fold in fruit and pecans and pour batter into sprayed, floured tube pan. Bake for 2 hours 30 minutes to 2 hours 45 minutes. Test after 2 hours 30 minutes. Cool and remove carefully from pan.

BAKE SALE TIP:

Present cake in a large 30-inch (70 cm) piece of clear plastic wrap. Pull all sides up about 8 or 10 inches. Squeeze the ends about 3 inches (8 cm) from top and tie with a big red bow.

Orange-Date Cake

4 cups flour	1 L
1 teaspoon baking soda	5 ml
1 cup (2 sticks) butter, softened	240 ml
2½ cups sugar	600 ml
4 eggs	
1½ cups buttermilk	360 ml
1 teaspoon orange extract	5 ml
1 tablespoon grated orange rind	15 ml
1 (11 ounce) can mandarin oranges	312 g
1 (8 ounce) package chopped dates	227 g
1 cup chopped pecans	240 ml

Glaze:

½ cup orange juice	120 ml
1¼ cups sugar	300 ml
1 teaspoon orange rind	5 ml
½ teaspoon orange extract	2 ml

- Preheat oven to 350° (176° C).

- Sift flour and baking soda and set aside. With mixer, beat butter and sugar, add eggs 1 at a time and beat well. Add buttermilk and dry ingredients alternately, ending with dry ingredients. Add orange extract and rind and beat well. Stir in oranges, dates and pecans.

- Pour into sprayed, floured bundt pan and bake for 1 hour 15 minutes or until toothpick inserted in center comes out clean. Do not remove pan.

- Mix orange juice, sugar, orange rind and extract. Bring to a boil and cool. Pour glaze slowly over cake while still in pan.

Pecan Cake

1 (18 ounce) box butter-pecan cake mix	510 g
½ cup (1 stick) butter, melted	120 ml
3 eggs, divided	
1 cup chopped pecans	240 ml
1 (8 ounce) package cream cheese, softened	227 g
1 (1 pound) box powdered sugar	.5 kg

- Preheat oven to 350° (176° C).

- Combine cake mix, ¾ cup (180 ml) water, butter and 1 egg and beat on medium speed for 1 minute. Stir in pecans and pour into 9 x 13-inch (23 x 33 cm) sprayed, floured foil baking pan.

- With mixer, beat cream cheese until creamy and add 2 eggs and powdered sugar. Beat until they blend well. Spread over cake. Bake for 40 minutes or until toothpick inserted in center comes out clean.

BAKE SALE TIP:

When cake cools, add some color to this presentation by sprinkling a handful of M&M® minis on top. This cake doesn't need any more "sweet", so just a handful will do. Wrap with plastic wrap. Transport cake in foil pan on level baking sheet so top will not crack.

Peppy Poppy Seed Bundt Cake

1 (18 ounce) package yellow cake mix   510 g
1 (3.4 ounce) package instant
    coconut-cream pudding mix   98 g
½ cup oil   120 ml
3 eggs
2 tablespoons poppy seeds   30 ml

- Preheat oven to 350° (176° C).

- Combine cake mix, pudding mix, 1 cup (240 ml) water, oil and eggs and beat on low speed until moist. Increase speed to medium for 2 minutes.

- Stir in poppy seeds. Pour into sprayed, floured bundt pan.

- Bake for 50 minutes or until toothpick inserted in center comes out clean.

- Cool for 10 minutes then remove from pan. Dust with powdered sugar using a flour sifter.

Pineapple Cake

2 eggs, beaten	
2 cups sugar	480 ml
1 (20 ounce) can crushed pineapple with juice	567 g
2 cups flour	480 ml
2 teaspoons baking soda	10 ml
1 teaspoon vanilla	5 ml
1 cup chopped pecans	240 ml
1 (16 ounce) can cream cheese icing	.5 kg

- Preheat oven to 350° (176° C).

- Combine beaten eggs, sugar and pineapple in large bowl. Stir in flour, baking soda, vanilla and pecans.

- Pour into 9 x 13-inch (23 x 33 cm) sprayed, floured foil baking pan and bake for 35 to 40 minutes. After cake cools completely, spread icing over cake.

Praline-Pear Cake

2½ cups flour	600 ml
1½ cups sugar	360 ml
1½ teaspoons baking soda	7 ml
¼ teaspoon baking powder	1 ml
1½ teaspoons ground cinnamon	7 ml
½ teaspoon ground cloves	2 ml
½ cup shortening	120 ml
1 (29 ounce) can pear halves, drained, pureed	805 g
2 eggs	
⅔ cup golden raisins	160 ml

Praline Topping:

1⅓ cups packed brown sugar	320 ml
½ cup (1 stick) butter	120 ml
⅓ cup half-and-half cream	80 ml
¾ cup flaked coconut	180 ml
1 cup chopped pecans	240 ml

- Preheat oven to 350° (176° C). Combine flour, sugar, baking soda, baking powder, cinnamon, ½ teaspoon (2 ml) salt and cloves in mixing bowl. Add shortening, pureed pears and eggs and beat on low speed for 30 seconds. Increase speed to medium and beat another 3 minutes. Fold in raisins and pour into 9 x 13-inch (23 x 33 cm) sprayed, floured foil baking pan. Bake for 40 to 45 minutes. Cake is done when toothpick inserted in center comes out clean.

- For topping, mix brown sugar, butter and half-and-half in medium saucepan. Bring to a boil and stir constantly. Remove from burner and stir in coconut and pecans. Spread over warm cake.

Pumpkin Cake

3 eggs	
2 cups sugar	480 ml
1 (15 ounce) can pumpkin	425 g
1 cup oil	240 ml
2 cups flour	480 ml
1 teaspoon baking soda	5 ml
2 teaspoons baking powder	10 ml
2 teaspoons cinnamon	10 ml
½ teaspoon ginger	2 ml
½ teaspoon cloves	2 ml
½ teaspoon nutmeg	2 ml

Frosting:

1 (3 ounce) package cream cheese, softened	84 g
6 tablespoons (¾ stick) butter, softened	90 ml
3 cups powdered sugar	710 ml
1 teaspoon vanilla	5 ml
1 tablespoon milk	15 ml

- Preheat oven to 350° (176° C).

- In mixing bowl, beat eggs, sugar, pumpkin and oil.

- Add flour, baking soda, baking powder, spices and ½ teaspoon (2 ml) salt and mix well.

- Pour into 9 x 13-inch (23 x 33 cm) sprayed, floured foil baking pan. Bake for 30 to 35 minutes. Cake is done when toothpick inserted in center comes out clean.

- With mixer, beat cream cheese and butter until creamy. Stir in powdered sugar, vanilla and milk and add a little more milk if frosting is too stiff. Pour over hot cake.

Pumpkin-Rum Cake

1 (18 ounce) box white cake mix	510 g
1 (15 ounce) can pumpkin	425 g
3 eggs	
½ cup rum	120 ml
¾ cup chopped pecans, toasted	180 ml

- Preheat oven to 325° (162° C).

- In large bowl, combine dry cake mix, pumpkin, eggs and rum. Beat on low speed to blend. Increase speed and beat 2 minutes more.

- Fold in pecans and pour batter into 12-cup (3 L) sprayed, floured bundt pan.

- Bake for 45 to 50 minutes.

- Cool 10 minutes. Invert onto serving platter and frost with Orange Glaze.

Orange Glaze:

1 cup powdered sugar	240 ml
2 tablespoons plus ½ teaspoon orange juice	30 ml/2 ml
1 tablespoon orange zest	15 ml

- Mix all ingredients until smooth.

- Pour over cake allowing glaze to run down sides.

BAKE SALE TIP:

Sprinkle a few "corn candies" or pineapple- papaya-mango tropical fruits on cake.

Spiced Pear Cake

1 (15 ounce) can sliced pears, drained	425 g
1 (18 ounce) box carrot cake mix	510 g
3 eggs	
⅓ cup oil	80 ml
1 teaspoon ground cinnamon	5 ml
1 teaspoon ginger	5 ml
1 cup chopped pecans, divided	240 ml
¾ cup cream cheese icing	
(from 16 ounce carton)	180 ml/.5 kg

- Preheat oven to 350° (176° C).

- Dry pear slices well with paper towels and chop coarsely.

- In bowl, combine cake mix, eggs, oil, spices and ¾ cup (180 ml) water and stir until smooth. Stir in chopped pears and ⅔ cup (160 ml) pecans.

- Pour into 10-inch (25 cm) sprayed bundt pan. Bake for 40 to 45 minutes. Cake is done when toothpick inserted in center comes out clean. Cool in pan about 15 minutes. Invert cake onto rack, remove pan and cool completely.

- When cake cools, place icing in glass measuring cup and microwave on HIGH for 15 seconds. Slowly drizzle over cake and allow some icing to drip down sides.

Surprise Cake

5 tablespoons (⅔ stick) butter	75 ml
1 (16 ounce) box dry coconut-pecan frosting mix	.5 kg
1 cup uncooked oats	240 ml
1 cup sour cream	240 ml
4 eggs	
1½ cups mashed bananas	360 ml
1 (18 ounce) box yellow cake mix	510 g

- Preheat oven to 350° (176° C).

- In saucepan, melt butter, stir in frosting mix and oats until crumbly and set aside.

- In large mixing bowl, blend sour cream, eggs and bananas until smooth.

- Fold in cake mix and beat 2 minutes.

- Pour 2 cups (480 ml) batter into sprayed, floured tube pan. Sprinkle with 1 cup (240 ml) crumb mixture. Repeat twice with batter and crumbs, ending with crumb mixture.

- Bake for 55 to 60 minutes. Cool in pan for 15 minutes.

- Remove from pan and invert cake so crumb mixture is on top.

Vanilla Wafer Cake

1 cup (2 sticks) butter, softened	240 ml
2¼ cups sugar	540 ml
6 eggs, slightly beaten	
1 (12 ounce) package vanilla wafer cookies	340 g
½ cup milk	120 ml
1 cup flaked coconut	240 ml
1 cup chopped pecans	240 ml
1 (16 ounce) carton coconut-pecan icing	.5 kg

- Preheat oven to 325° (162° C).

- Cream butter and sugar, add eggs, 1 at a time and beat after each addition.

- Crush wafers with rolling pin into fine crumbs. Stir in crumbs and milk alternately to egg-sugar mixture. Fold in coconut and pecans and pour into sprayed, floured tube pan.

- Bake for 1 hour 30 minutes. Cool in pan about 15 minutes. Remove cake from pan and cool completely. Ice cake with coconut-pecan icing.

Chocolate-Cookie Cake

1 (18 ounce) box white cake mix	510 g
⅓ cup oil	80 ml
4 egg whites	
1¾ cups coarsely chopped chocolate-sandwich cookies, divided	300 ml
1 cup chopped pecans	240 ml

Frosting:

4¼ cups powdered sugar	1 L
1 cup (2 sticks) butter, softened	240 ml
1 cup shortening	240 ml
1 teaspoon almond flavoring	5 ml

• Preheat oven to 350° (176° C).

• Combine cake mix, oil, 1¼ cups (300 ml) water and egg whites with mixer and blend on low speed until moist. Beat 2 minutes at high speed.

• Gently fold in 1¼ cups (300 ml) cookie crumbs and chopped pecans. Set remaining cookie crumbs aside. Pour batter evenly into 2 (9-inch/23 cm) sprayed, floured round cake pans.

• Bake for 25 to 30 minutes or until toothpick inserted in center comes out clean. Cool for 15 minutes and remove from pan. Cool completely before frosting.

• For frosting combine remaining ingredients with mixer and beat until creamy.

• Spread some frosting on first layer, place second cake on top and spread remaining frosting on top and sides.

• Sprinkle with remaining ½ cup (120 ml) crushed chocolate-sandwich cookies.

Chocolate-Hurricane Cake

This is easy and very yummy.

1 cup chopped pecans	240 ml
1 (3 ounce) can flaked coconut	84 g
1 (18 ounce) box German chocolate cake mix	510 g
⅓ cup oil	80 ml
3 eggs	
½ cup (1 stick) butter, melted	120 ml
1 (8 ounce) package cream cheese, softened	227 g
1 (16 ounce) box powdered sugar	.5 kg

* Preheat oven to 350° (176° C).

* Spray 9 x 13-inch (23 x 33 cm) foil baking pan and cover bottom of pan with pecans and coconut.

* In mixing bowl, combine cake mix, 1¼ cups (300 ml) water, oil and eggs and beat well. Carefully pour batter over pecans and coconut.

* In mixing bowl, combine butter, cream cheese and powdered sugar and whip to blend. Spoon mixture over batter and bake for 40 to 42 minutes. (You cannot test for doneness with toothpick because cake will appear sticky even when it is done.) The icing sinks into bottom as it bakes and forms white ribbon inside.

BAKE SALE TIP:

This is so easy to make! Just bake it in a 9 x 13-inch (23 x 33 cm) foil pan and all you have to do is wrap it with plastic wrap.

Double Chocolate-Pecan Cake

1 (18 ounce) box devil's food cake mix	510 g
½ cup oil	120 ml
1 teaspoon ground cinnamon	5 ml
3 eggs, slightly beaten	
1 teaspoon rum extract	5 ml
¾ cup finely chopped pecans	180 ml
1 (16 ounce) carton triple-chocolate fudge icing	.5 kg
1 cup white chocolate chips	240 ml

- Preheat oven to 350° (176° C).

- In large bowl, beat cake mix ingredients, 1⅓ cups (320 ml) water, oil, cinnamon and eggs. Beat on medium speed 2 minutes and scrape bowl occasionally.

- Stir in rum extract and pecans and pour into 9 x 13-inch (23 x 33 cm) sprayed, floured foil pan.

- Bake for 35 to 38 minutes or until toothpick inserted in center comes out clean. Cool completely.

- Spread fudge icing over top of cake and sprinkle white chocolate chips on top of icing.

BAKE SALE TIP:

Cover with light colored sheet plastic wrap and transport on level baking sheet.

Oreo® Cake

Is this cake great? And who doesn't like
Oreos®? My son's favorite cake was always white
cake and white icing – that is until I made this cake.

1 (18 ounce) box white cake mix	510 g
⅓ cup oil	80 ml
4 egg whites	
1¾ cups coarsely chopped Oreo® cookies,	
divided	420 ml
1 (16 ounce) carton fluffy white icing	.5 kg

- Preheat oven to 325° (162° C).

- In mixing bowl, combine cake mix, oil, 1¼ cups (300 ml) water and egg whites. Blend on low speed until moist, then beat for 2 minutes on high speed. Fold in 1¼ cups (300 ml) chopped cookies and pour batter into 10-inch (25 cm) sprayed, floured tube pan.

- Bake for 1 hour or until toothpick inserted in center comes out clean. Cool for 15 minutes, remove from pan and cool completely.

- Spread icing over top and parts of sides of cake and sprinkle remaining chopped cookies on top of cake.

- Let icing set several hours before wrapping cake in plastic wrap.

Turtle Cake

1 (18 ounce) box German chocolate cake mix	510 g
½ cup (1 stick) butter, softened	120 ml
½ cup oil	120 ml
1 (14 ounce) can sweetened, condensed milk,	
divided	396 g
1 (1 pound) bag caramels	.5 kg
1 cup chopped pecans	240 ml

Icing:

½ cup (1 stick) butter	120 ml
3 tablespoons cocoa	45 ml
6 tablespoons evaporated milk	90 ml
1 (16 ounce) box powdered sugar	.5 kg
1 teaspoon vanilla	5 ml

- Preheat oven to 350° (176° C).

- Combine cake mix, butter, 1½ cups (360 ml) water, oil and half sweetened condensed milk. Pour half batter into 9 x 13-inch (23 x 33 cm) sprayed foil pan and bake for 20 minutes.

- Melt caramels and blend with remaining sweetened condensed milk. Spread evenly over baked cake layer and sprinkle with pecans. Cover with remaining batter and bake an additional 20 to 25 minutes.

- Melt butter in saucepan and mix in cocoa and milk. Add powdered sugar and vanilla to mixture and blend well. Spread over cake.

  TIP: Transfer cake on a level cookie sheet to keep frosting from cracking.

White Chocolate-Almond Cake

1 (18 ounce) box white cake mix	510 g
4 egg whites	
¼ cup oil	60 ml
1 teaspoon almond extract	5 ml
1 cup slivered, chopped almonds	240 ml
6 (1 ounce) squares white chocolate, melted	6 (28 g)
1 (16 ounce) carton caramel icing	.5 kg

- Preheat oven to 350° (176° C).

- In mixing bowl, combine cake mix, egg whites, oil, almond extract and 1½ cups (360 ml) water and beat until they blend well.

- Stir in chopped almonds and melted white chocolate and pour into 2 (9-inch/23 cm) round cake pans.

- Bake for 30 to 35 minutes.

- Spread each layer with half caramel icing. Stack layers.

BAKE SALE TIP:

Since this cake has white chocolate in it, add a nice touch with swirled semi-sweet and white chocolate morsels over the cake. They are available in 10-ounce (280 g) packages, but you will only need about ⅓ cup (80 ml). Eat the rest or decorate another cake. They are pretty over chocolate icing too.

Black Russian Cake

1 (18 ounce) box milk-chocolate cake mix	510 g
½ cup oil	120 ml
1 (3.9 ounce) package instant chocolate pudding mix	114 g
4 eggs, room temperature	
⅔ cup strong brewed coffee	160 ml
⅓ cup creme de cacao liqueur	80 ml

Icing:

1½ cups powdered sugar	360 ml
2 tablespoons (¼ stick) butter, melted	30 ml
Coffee liqueur	

- Preheat oven to 350° (176° C).

- In mixing bowl, combine cake mix, oil, pudding mix, eggs, coffee and creme de cacao liqueur.

- Beat for 4 to 5 minutes and pour into sprayed, floured bundt pan. Bake for 55 to 60 minutes. Cool.

- For icing, combine powdered sugar and melted butter. Add coffee liqueur a little at a time, until it reaches spreading consistency, but thin enough to run down sides. Serves 20.

BAKE SALE TIP:

Write a little note on your bake sale tag: "This is great with a big scoop of vanilla ice cream on top."

Quick-N-Easy Cherry Cake

1 (18 ounce) box French vanilla cake mix	510 g
½ cup (1 stick) butter, melted	120 ml
2 eggs	
1 (20 ounce) can cherry pie filling	567 g
1 cup chopped pecans	240 ml
Powdered sugar	

- Preheat oven to 350° (176° C).

- Mix all ingredients by hand in large bowl.

- Pour into sprayed, floured bundt pan.

- Bake for 1 hour. Sprinkle top of cake with powdered sugar.

Lemon Poppy Seed Cake

1 (18 ounce) box lemon pudding cake mix	510 g
1 (8 ounce) carton sour cream	227 g
3 eggs, slightly beaten	
⅓ cup oil	80 ml
⅓ cup poppy seeds	80 ml
Powdered sugar	

- Preheat oven to 350° (176° C).

- In mixing bowl, combine cake mix, sour cream, eggs, oil and ¼ cup (60 ml) water and beat on medium speed until they mix well. Stir in poppy seeds and mix well. Pour into 12-cup (3 L) sprayed, floured bundt pan.

- Bake for 45 to 55 minutes. Cake is done when toothpick inserted in center comes out clean. Cool. Dust cake with powdered sugar using a flour sifter.

Golden Rum Cake

1 (18 ounce) box yellow cake mix	
with pudding	510 g
3 eggs	
⅓ cup oil	80 ml
¼ cup plus 1 tablespoon rum, divided	60 ml/15 ml
1 cup chopped pecans	240 ml
1 (16 ounce) carton caramel icing	.5 kg

- Preheat oven to 325° (162° C).

- Mix cake mix, eggs, 1¼ cups (300 ml) water and ½ cup (120 ml) rum and blend well. Stir in pecans and pour into 10-inch (25 cm) sprayed, floured tube pan. Bake for 1 hour or until toothpick inserted in center comes out clean.

- Mix caramel icing with 1 tablespoon (15 ml) rum. Spread over cool cake.

Easy Cherry-Pineapple Cake

1 (20 ounce) can crushed pineapple, drained	567 g
1 (20 ounce) can cherry pie filling	567 g
1 (18 ounce) box yellow cake mix	510 g
1 cup (2 sticks) butter, softened	240 ml
1¼ cups chopped pecans	300 ml

- Preheat oven to 350° (176° C).
- Place all ingredients in mixing bowl and mix by hand.
- Pour into 9 x 13-inch (23 x 33 cm) sprayed, floured baking dish.
- Bake for 1 hour 10 minutes.

BAKE SALE TIP:

If you want to add something special to this cake, buy 1 (6 ounce/168 g) package premium candied pineapple, cut into smaller pieces and sprinkle over top.

Great Pound Cake

½ cup shortening	120 ml
1 cup (2 sticks) butter, softened	240 ml
3 cups sugar	710 ml
5 eggs	
3½ cups flour	830 ml
½ teaspoon baking powder	2 ml
1 cup milk	240 ml
1 teaspoon rum flavoring	5 ml
1 teaspoon coconut flavoring	5 ml

Glaze:

1 cup sugar	240 ml
½ teaspoon almond extract	2 ml

- Preheat oven to 325° (162° C).

- In mixing bowl, cream shortening, butter and sugar. Add eggs and beat for 4 minutes. Combine flour and baking powder. Add dry ingredients and milk alternately to butter mixture. Begin and end with flour. Add rum and coconut flavorings.

- Pour into large sprayed, floured tube pan and bake for 1 hour 35 minutes. Do not open door during baking.

- Right before cake is done, bring sugar and ⅓ cup (80 ml) water to a rolling boil. Remove from heat and add almond extract. While cake is still in pan, pour glaze over cake and cool for 30 minutes before removing from pan.

Strawberry Pound Cake

1 (18 ounce) box strawberry cake mix	510 g
1 (3.4 ounce) package instant pineapple pudding mix	100 g
⅓ cup oil	80 ml
4 eggs	
1 (3 ounce) package dry strawberry gelatin	84 g
1 (16 ounce) carton creamy strawberry icing	.5 kg

• Preheat oven to 350° (176° C).

• Combine ingredients plus 1 cup (240 ml) water in mixing bowl and beat for 2 minutes at medium speed.

• Pour into sprayed, floured tube pan.

• Bake for 55 to 60 minutes. Cake is done when toothpick inserted in center comes out clean.

• Cool for 20 minutes before removing cake from pan.

• Spread icing over top of cake.

TIP: Decorate (at the last minute) with fresh strawberries or red sprinkles.

Red Velvet Pound Cake

3 cups sugar	710 ml
¾ cup shortening	180 ml
6 eggs	
1 teaspoon vanilla	5 ml
3 cups flour	710 ml
1 cup milk	240 ml
2 (1 ounce) bottles red food coloring	2 (28 g)

Icing:

1 (3 ounce) package cream cheese, softened	84 g
¼ cup (½ stick) butter, softened	60 ml
3 tablespoons milk	45 ml
1 (1 pound) box powdered sugar	.5 kg
Red sprinkles	

- Preheat oven to 325° (162° C).

- Cream sugar and shortening. Add eggs, 1 at a time, and beat after each addition. Mix in vanilla. Add ¼ teaspoon (1 ml) salt, flour and milk alternating each, beginning and ending with flour. Add food coloring and beat until smooth.

- Bake in sprayed, floured tube pan for 1 hour 30 minutes. Cool in pan for 10 minutes. Remove cake from pan. Cool before frosting.

- Combine cream cheese, butter and milk and beat until smooth. Stir in powdered sugar, frost cake and top with red sprinkles.

Pumpkin Pie Pound Cake

*How could you miss with pumpkin pie and
pound cake all in one recipe?*

1 cup shortening	240 ml
1¼ cups sugar	300 ml
¾ cup packed brown sugar	180 ml
5 eggs, room temperature	
1 cup canned pumpkin	240 ml
2½ cups flour	600 ml
2 teaspoons cinnamon	10 ml
1 teaspoon ground nutmeg	5 ml
1 teaspoon baking soda	5 ml
½ cup orange juice, room temperature	120 ml
2 teaspoons vanilla	10 ml
1½ cups chopped pecans	360 ml
1 (16 ounce) carton creamy orange icing	.5 kg

- Preheat oven to 325° (162° C).

- Cream shortening and both sugars for 5 minutes.

- Add eggs, one at a time and mix well after each addition. Mix in pumpkin. In separate bowl, combine flour, spices, ½ teaspoon (2 ml) salt and baking soda.

- Gradually beat dry ingredients into batter until they mix well. Fold in orange juice, vanilla and chopped pecans.

- Pour into sprayed, floured tube pan.

- Bake for 1 hour 5 to 10 minutes. Cool cake in pan for 10 to 15 minutes then invert cake out onto rack. Cool completely. Spread icing over cooled cake.

Pineapple-Pound Cake

½ cup shortening	120 ml
1 cup (2 sticks) butter, softened	240 ml
2¾ cups sugar	660 ml
6 eggs	
3 cups flour	710 ml
1 teaspoon baking powder	5 ml
¼ cup milk	60 ml
1 teaspoon vanilla	5 ml
1 (8 ounce) can crushed pineapple with juice	227 g
1 cup chopped pecans	240 ml

Glaze:

¼ cup (½ stick) butter, softened	60 ml
1 (8 ounce) can crushed pineapple, well drained	227 g
1½ cups powdered sugar	360 ml

- Preheat oven to 325° (162° C).

- Combine shortening, butter and sugar in mixing bowl and beat well. Add eggs, 1 at a time and beat well. Add flour, ½ teaspoon (2 ml) salt and baking powder, alternately with milk, vanilla and crushed pineapple. Stir pecans.

- Spoon into 10-inch (25 cm) sprayed, floured tube pan and bake for 1 hour 20 minutes or when toothpick inserted in center comes out clean. Cool for 10 minutes before inverting onto cake plate. Cool completely.

- For glaze, mix all ingredients and spread over cake.

Peanut Butter Pound Cake

1 cup (2 sticks) butter	240 ml
2 cups sugar	480 ml
1 cup packed light brown sugar	240 ml
½ cup creamy peanut butter	120 ml
5 eggs	
1 tablespoon vanilla	15 ml
3 cups flour	710 ml
½ teaspoon baking powder	2 ml
½ teaspoon baking soda	2 ml
1 cup whipping cream	240 ml

Icing:

¼ cup (½ stick) butter, softened	60 ml
3 - 4 tablespoons milk	45 ml
⅓ cup creamy or chunky peanut butter	80 ml
1 (16 ounce) box powdered sugar	.5 kg

- Preheat oven to 350° (176° C).

- Cream butter, sugars and peanut butter and beat until fluffy. Add eggs 1 at a time and beat well after each addition. Add vanilla and blend. Sift dry ingredients with ½ teaspoon (2 ml) salt and add alternately with whipping cream.

- Pour mixture into large, sprayed, floured tube pan and bake for 1 hour 10 minutes or until toothpick inserted in center comes out clean.

- To make icing, combine all ingredients and beat until smooth. Frost cake.

Brown Sugar-Rum Cake

1½ cups (3 sticks) butter, softened	360 ml
1 (16 ounce) package brown sugar	.5 kg
1 cup sugar	240 ml
5 large eggs	
¾ cup milk	180 ml
¼ cup rum	60 ml
2 teaspoons vanilla	10 ml
3 cups flour	710 ml
2 teaspoons baking powder	10 ml
1½ cups chopped pecans	360 ml

- Preheat oven to 325° (162° C). With electric mixer, beat butter and both sugars at medium speed about 5 minutes.

- Add eggs, 1 at a time and beat just until yellow disappears.

- Combine milk, rum and vanilla in separate bowl. Combine flour, baking powder and ¼ teaspoon (1 ml) salt in another bowl. Add half flour mixture to butter and sugar and mix. Add milk mixture and mix.

- Add remaining flour mixture and beat at low speed. Fold in pecans and pour into sprayed, floured tube pan.

- Bake for 1 hour 25 minutes. Cake is done when toothpick inserted in center comes out clean.

- Cool in pan for 20 minutes, remove from pan and cool completely.

    TIP: If you don't want to use rum, just add ¼ cup (60 ml) milk and 2 teaspoons (10 ml) rum flavoring. Call it Brown Sugar Coffee Cake.

Glazed Chocolate Pound Cake

1 cup (2 sticks) butter, softened	240 ml
2 cups sugar	480 ml
1 cup firmly packed brown sugar	240 ml
6 large eggs	
2½ cups flour	600 ml
½ teaspoon baking soda	2 ml
½ cup cocoa	120 ml
1 (8 ounce) carton sour cream	227 g
2 teaspoons vanilla	10 ml

Glaze:

1 cup sugar	240 ml
½ teaspoon almond extract	2 ml

- Preheat oven to 325° (162° C).

- Combine butter and both sugars in mixing bowl. Beat with electric mixer about 2 minutes until soft and creamy. Add eggs and beat well.

- Combine flour, baking soda and cocoa alternately with sour cream and vanilla. End with flour mixture. Mix at lowest speed until mixture blends after each addition. Pour batter into 10-inch (25 cm) sprayed, floured tube pan and bake for 1 hour 20 minutes.

- Prepare glaze when cake is almost done. Bring sugar and ⅓ cup (80 ml) water to a rolling boil. Remove from heat and add almond extract. Drizzle glaze over cake. Let stand about 30 minutes before removing from pan.

Easy Blueberry Pound Cake

1 (18 ounce) box yellow cake mix	567 g
1 (8 ounce) package cream cheese, softened	227 g
½ cup oil	120 ml
4 eggs	
1 (15 ounce) can whole blueberries, drained	425 g
Powdered sugar	

- Preheat oven to 350° (176° C).

- Beat all ingredients with mixer for 3 minutes. Pour into sprayed, floured bundt or tube pan.

- Bake for 50 minutes. Cake is done when toothpick inserted in center comes out clean.

- Sprinkle top of cake with powdered sugar.

Coconut-Pecan Pound Cake

1 cup flaked coconut	240 ml
1 (18 ounce) box carrot cake mix	510 g
⅓ cup oil	80 ml
3 eggs, slightly beaten	
1 teaspoon vanilla	5 ml
¾ cup finely chopped pecans	180 ml
½ (16 ounce) carton coconut-pecan icing	½ (.5 kg)

- Preheat oven to 350° (176° C).

- Prepare 12-cup (3 L) bundt pan with shortening and a little flour. (Do not use cooking spray.) In shallow baking pan, spread coconut and bake about 4 to 5 minutes, stirring occasionally, until a light golden brown. Set aside 2 tablespoons (30 ml) for garnish.

- In mixing bowl, combine cake mix, 1¼ cups (300 ml) water, oil, eggs and vanilla and beat with mixer on low for 30 seconds. Increase speed and beat on medium speed for 2 minutes.

- Fold in pecans and coconut (except 2 tablespoons/ 30 ml) and spoon into bundt pan. Bake for 40 to 43 minutes or until toothpick inserted in center comes out clean. Cool at least 1 to 2 hours.

- Place icing in small bowl, add 1 teaspoon (5 ml) water and microwave about 8 seconds or until thin enough to drizzle. Drizzle over top of cake, let just a little run down sides and sprinkle on remaining 2 tablespoons (30 ml) coconut.

Chocolate Pound Cake

3 cups sugar	710 ml
1 cup (2 sticks) butter, softened	240 ml
½ cup shortening	120 ml
5 eggs	
3 cups flour	710 ml
½ cup cocoa	120 ml
½ teaspoon baking powder	2 ml
1 cup milk	240 ml
1 teaspoon vanilla	5 ml
Powdered sugar	

- Preheat oven to 350° (176° C).

- Use electric mixer to cream sugar, butter and shortening at medium speed. Add eggs, 1 at a time, and beat well after each addition.

- Sift flour, cocoa, baking powder and ¼ teaspoon (1 ml) salt. Reduce speed to low and add half of dry ingredients. Add milk and vanilla and beat well. Add remaining flour and beat well.

- Pour into 10-inch (25 cm) sprayed, floured bundt pan and bake for 1 hour 20 minutes. Cool for 10 minutes in pan, turn on rack or plate to cool and sprinkle powdered sugar over top.

BAKE SALE TIP:

Let cake rest several hours before wrapping in plastic wrap.

Brandied Cherries for Angel Food Cake

You cannot beat this simple dessert when you want to enjoy ripe cherries in the peak of the season. If you like, add 1 or 2 chopped apricots with the cherries for a little variety.

½ cup sugar	120 ml
¼ cup brandy	60 ml
2 pounds cherries, pitted	1 kg
2 tablespoons lemon juice	30 ml

- Combine sugar and brandy in medium saucepan.

- Add cherries and lemon juice. Bring to simmer and stir occasionally until sugar dissolves. Cook cherries over medium heat until tender, about 5 minutes.

BAKE SALE TIP:

Double this recipe and pour into half-pint jelly jars. Cut 6-inch (15 cm) rounds of colorful fabric. Place flat lid on jar, cover with fabric and screw on lid rims.

Be sure to write a note on your bake sale to serve warm over ice cream or angel food cake.

There are many commercial icings available today and the ones I have tried are good. There are also good, easy and quick icings you can whip up in no time. Here are delicious icing recipes that will work on most cakes, bars or squares you make. Try one – you'll like it.

Nutty Butter Cream Icing

1 (3 ounce) package cream cheese, softened	84 g
6 tablespoons (¾ stick) butter, softened	90 ml
1 tablespoon milk	15 ml
1 teaspoon vanilla	5 ml
2 cups powdered sugar	480 ml
½ cup chopped pecans	120 ml

• Beat cream cheese and butter. Stir in milk, vanilla, powdered sugar and pecans.

Sweet Butter Cream Icing

1 (8 ounce) package cream cheese, softened	227 g
½ cup (1 stick) butter, softened	120 ml
2 cups powdered sugar	480 ml
1 teaspoon vanilla	5 ml

• Beat cream cheese and butter and stir in powdered sugar and vanilla.

Completely Coco-Nutty Icing

1½ cups sugar	360 ml
6 tablespoons (¾ stick) butter	90 ml
1 cup sweetened condensed milk	240 ml
1 cup each chopped pecans and flaked coconut	240 ml

• Combine sugar, butter and condensed milk in saucepan and bring to a boil. Boil 2 minutes and stir in pecans and coconut.

Hot 'N Creamy Crunch Icing

6 tablespoons milk	90 ml
½ cup (1 stick) butter	120 ml
⅓ cup cocoa	80 ml
1 (16 ounce) box powdered sugar	.5 kg
1 teaspoon vanilla	5 ml
½ cup chopped pecans	120 ml

• Combine milk, butter and cocoa in saucepan, bring to a boil over medium heat and stir often. Remove from heat, stir in powdered sugar and vanilla until smooth. Add pecans and mix well.

Marshmallow-Heaven Icing

1 cup (2 sticks) butter, softened	240 ml
1 (7 ounce) jar marshmallow cream	198 g
2 cups powdered sugar	480 ml
1 teaspoon vanilla	5 ml

• With mixer on low speed, beat all ingredients until they blend. Increase speed to high and continue beating 2 more minutes until smooth and fluffy.

BAKE SALE TIP:

Goody Bag

Hold the bake sale around a holiday, a theme or special event such as Christmas, Halloween or a neighbor block party. Find seasonal items for props to reinforce your theme and have that special artist of the group arrange the food items.

2-Layer Cake Icing

1½ cups sugar	360 ml
½ cup (1 stick) butter	120 ml
1 (5 ounce) can evaporated milk	143 g
1 cup chopped pecans	240 ml
1 (3 ounce) can flaked coconut, optional	84 g
1 teaspoon vanilla	5 ml

• Mix sugar, butter and evaporated milk together in saucepan, boil 4 minutes and stir constantly. Remove from heat and add pecans, coconut and vanilla. Spread over hot bars or squares.

Creamy 2-Layer Cake Icing

¾ cup (1½ sticks) butter, softened	180 ml
1½ (8 ounce) packages cream cheese, softened	1½ (227 g)
1 teaspoon vanilla	5 ml
1½ teaspoons almond extract	7 ml
1½ - 2 (16 ounce) boxes powdered sugar	1½ (.5 kg)

• With mixer, cream butter and cream cheese until they blend well and are smooth. Stir in vanilla and almond extract and gradually add as much powdered sugar as needed for spreading evenly over layers and sides of cake.

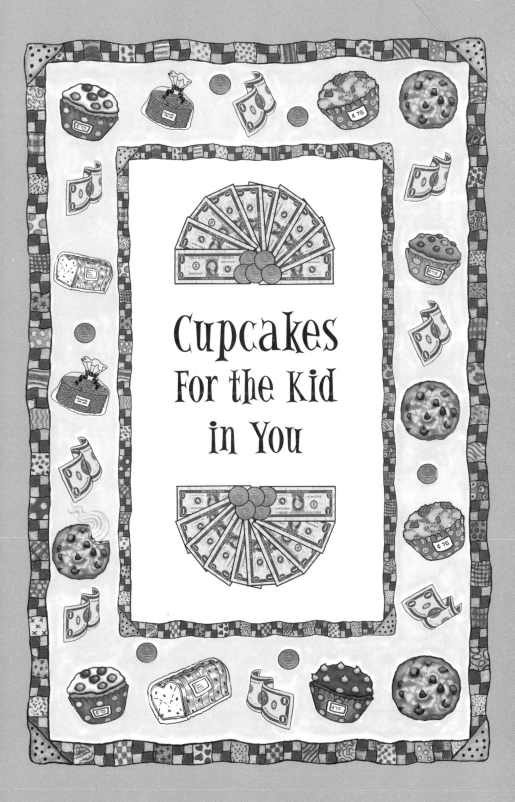

Cupcakes
For the Kid
in You

Caramel-Apple Cupcakes

1 (18 ounce) package carrot cake mix	510 g
3 cups peeled, chopped tart apples	710 ml
1 (12 ounce) package butterscotch chips	340 g
1 cup finely chopped pecans	240 ml

- Preheat oven to 350° (176° C).

- Make cake batter according to package directions. Fold in apples. Fill 12 sprayed or paper-lined jumbo muffin cups three-fourths full. Bake for 20 minutes or until toothpick inserted in center comes out clean.

- In saucepan on very low heat, melt butterscotch chips. Spread over cupcakes and sprinkle with chopped pecans.

Pumpkin Cupcakes

1 (18 ounce) box spice cake mix	510 g
1 (15 ounce) can pumpkin	425 g
3 eggs	
⅓ cup oil	80 ml
1 (16 ounce) carton caramel icing	.5 kg
½ cup finely chopped pecans	120 ml

- Preheat oven to 350° (176° C).

- With mixer, blend cake mix, pumpkin, eggs, oil and ⅓ cup (80 ml) water and beat for 2 minutes.

- Pour batter three-fourths full into 24 paper-lined muffin cups. Bake for 18 to 20 minutes or until toothpick inserted in center comes out clean. When cupcakes cool, ice with caramel icing and sprinkle chopped pecans over top.

Butter Pecan Cupcakes

1 (18 ounce) box butter pecan cake mix	510 g
⅓ cup oil	80 ml
3 eggs, slightly beaten	
½ cup finely chopped pecans	120 ml

Glaze:

1 tablespoon butter, softened	15 ml
2 tablespoons maple syrup	30 ml
⅓ cup powdered sugar	80 ml
¼ cup very finely chopped pecans	60 ml

- Preheat oven to 350° (176° C).

- Beat cake mix, 1 cup (240 ml) water, and beaten eggs for 2 minutes on low speed. Stir in pecans.

- Pour two-thirds batter into 24 muffin cups with paper linings and bake for 22 to 25 minutes or until toothpick inserted in center comes out clean.

- For glaze, combine butter, maple syrup and powdered sugar and beat thoroughly. Stir in pecans and drizzle over hot cupcakes.

In-Your-Face Cupcakes

1 (18 ounce) box classic white cake mix   510 g
⅓ cup oil   80 ml
3 eggs, slightly beaten
1 (16 ounce) carton butter-cream icing   .5 kg
Mini candy-coated chocolate candies

- Preheat oven to 350° (176° C).

- Blend cake mix, oil, eggs and 1 cup (240 ml) water and
  beat at low speed for 2 minutes.

- Place paper liners into 18 muffin cups and spoon
  mixture two-thirds full into each cup. Bake for
  20 minutes and test for doneness. Remove from oven
  and cool cupcakes on wire rack.

- Spread butter-cream icing over each cupcake and
  make a "face" with candy eyes, nose and big smile.
  Place on doily-lined plastic plate.

BAKE SALE TIP:

*To wrap for bake sale, cut 30-inch (70 cm) pieces of
plastic wrap and place plate in center. Pull plastic
wrap up about 10-inches (25 cm), pinch together and
tie with a colorful ribbon. This will keep icing from
touching wrap.*

*Cupcakes deserve decoration. Fun and fancy will sell faster than
plain. People want to buy what they don't want to make.*

Raspberry-Cream Cupcakes

1 (18 ounce) box white cake mix	510 g
1 (8 ounce) carton sour cream	227 g
½ cup oil	120 ml
2 eggs, slightly beaten	
4 tablespoons raspberry preserves	60 ml
1 (3 ounce) package cream cheese	84 g
1 (16 ounce) carton cream cheese frosting	.5 kg
Sliced fresh raspberries	

• Preheat oven to 350° (176° C).

• In large bowl, mix cake mix, sour cream, oil, ½ cup (120 ml) water and eggs with spoon. Mix until they blend well. Batter will be thick. Place paper lining cups into 2 (12-cup/3 L) muffin pans and divide batter evenly among muffin cups.

• In small bowl, stir raspberry preserves until fairly smooth. Cut cream cheese into 24 pieces and place 1 piece cream cheese on top of each cupcake and gently press down.

• Place about ½ teaspoon (2 ml) preserves over cream cheese and bake for 20 to 24 minutes. Cool completely for 30 minutes to 1 hour.

• Frost with cream cheese frosting and with 1 slice raspberry on top. Chill until bake sale.

BAKE SALE TIP:

Place 12 cupcakes on 2 round, foil pizza pans. Cut 2 (30-inch/70 cm) pieces of clear plastic wrap and place each pan in center. Pull ends up and tie with colorful ribbon.

Surprise Cupcakes

These cupcakes are great and you don't have to frost them.

1 (8 ounce) package cream cheese, softened	227 g
¾ cup plus 1⅓ cups sugar, divided	180 ml/ 320 ml
1 egg, slightly beaten	
1 cup chocolate chips	240 ml
¼ cup cocoa	60 ml
1½ cups flour	360 ml
1 teaspoon baking soda	5 ml
⅓ cup oil	80 ml
½ cup slivered almonds	120 ml

- Preheat oven to 350° (176° C).

- With mixer, combine cream cheese, ½ cup (120 ml) sugar and egg and beat until mixture is smooth; stir in chocolate chips.

- In bowl combine cocoa, 1⅓ cups (320 ml) sugar, flour, baking soda, pinch of salt, oil and 1 cup (240 ml) water and stir by hand. Mix well, but not too vigorously.

- Fill 18 muffin cups with paper linings half full and place 1 heaping tablespoon (15 ml) cream cheese mixture over each muffin. Use all cream cheese mixture.

- Sprinkle each muffin with slivered almonds and a little extra sugar and bake for 20 to 25 minutes or until toothpick inserted in center comes out clean. Remove cupcake from pan while muffins are still hot. Cool on rack.

Cheesecake-Fruit Cupcakes

2 (7 ounce) packages strawberry-cheesecake muffin mix	2 (198 g)
1 cup milk	240 ml
¾ cup chopped pecans	180 ml
1 (16 ounce) carton strawberry icing	.5 kg
¾ cup cherry flavored Craisins® (dried cranberries)	180 ml

- Preheat oven to 400° (204° C).

- Combine muffin mix and milk in bowl and mix by hand until they blend well. Stir in pecans and spoon two-thirds full into 12 muffin cups with paper linings.

- Bake for 15 minutes or until toothpick inserted in center comes out clean. Cool.

- Spread with strawberry icing and sprinkle 3 to 5 cranberries on top of each cupcake.

BAKE SALE TIP:

I have found many plastic plates, platters, bowls, etc. for a dollar or less at discount and hobby stores. Before you place cupcakes on platter, line plates with pretty doilies. You can find doilies of all sizes in white, gold and silver.

Fun Cupcakes

1 (18 ounce) box white cake mix	510 g
⅓ cup oil	80 ml
3 eggs, beaten	
30 flat-bottom ice cream cones	
1 (16 ounce) carton confetti icing	.5 kg
About ½ cup fruit Skittles® candies	120 ml

- Preheat oven to 325° (162° C).

- Prepare cake mix according to package directions using oil, eggs and 1 cup (240 ml) water. Place ice cream cones in 2 (12 cup/3 L) muffin pans on baking sheet and fill each cone with a scant two-thirds full of batter. Bake for 25 to 30 minutes and cool completely.

- Frost each fun cake with confetti icing and sprinkle about 3 to 5 Skittles® on top of each cupcake.

BAKE SALE TIP:

If at all possible, turn you bake sale into a social event with live music, food demonstrations, games or a clown that ties balloons into animals. Make it a tradition so people will expect the event every year!

Fancy Cone Cakes

1 (18 ounce) box yellow cake mix	510 g
3 eggs	
⅓ cup oil	80 ml
1 (2.6 ounce, 18 count) box flat-bottom,	
colored ice cream cones	70 g
1 (16 ounce) carton rainbow chip icing	.5 kg
About ½ cup tropical trio dried fruit	120 ml
About ½ cup fruit Skittles®	120 ml
Green cake coloring	
M&M's®	

- Preheat oven to 325° (162° C).

- Prepare cake mix according to package directions using 3 eggs, oil and 1 cup (240 ml) water; beat well. Spoon two- thirds filling in 18 pink, green and brown colored ice cream cones. Place cones in muffin cups and bake for 25 to 30 minutes. Cool completely.

- Spread some icing on pink and green cones. Sprinkle some pink colored tropical fruit on 6 pink cones.

- Place about ¾ cup (180 ml) icing in small bowl, add a drop of green coloring and mix well.

- Ice 6 green cones and sprinkle some green Skittles® on top. Ice chocolate cones and place some M&M's® on top.

Triple-Chocolate Cones

1 (19 ounce) box classic fudge brownies	538 g
½ cup oil	120 ml
2 eggs	
1 (2.6 ounce, 18 count) box ice cream cones	70 g
1 (16 ounce) carton prepared triple chocolate fudge icing	.5 kg
1 (8 ounce) package vanilla-yogurt raisins	227 g

- Preheat oven to 325° (162° C).

- Combine brownie mix, oil, eggs and ¼ cup (60 ml) water and mix well. Place ice cream cones in muffin cups to bake.

- Carefully spoon batter into ice cream cones and fill two-thirds full. Bake for 25 minutes or until toothpick inserted in center comes out clean. Cool completely.

- Spread icing on each cone and sprinkle several yogurt raisins on top.

Bye-Bye
Bake Sale
Pies

Chess Pie

½ cup (1 stick) butter, softened   120 ml
2 cups sugar   480 ml
1 tablespoon cornstarch   15 ml
4 eggs
1 (9-inch) frozen piecrust

- Preheat oven to 325° (162° C).

- Cream butter, sugar and cornstarch. Add eggs, 1 at a time, and beat well after each addition.

- Pour mixture in piecrust. Cover piecrust edges with strips of foil to prevent excessive browning.

- Bake for 45 minutes or until center is firm.

Chocolate-Coconut Pie

1½ cups flaked coconut   360 ml
1½ cups chopped pecans   360 ml
1 (12 ounce) package chocolate chips   340 g
1 (6 ounce) graham cracker piecrust   168 g
1 (14 ounce) can sweetened condensed milk 396 g

- Preheat oven to 350° (176° C).

- Combine coconut, pecans and chocolate chips. Sprinkle mixture over piecrust.

- Pour sweetened condensed milk evenly over coconut mixture.

- Bake for 25 to 30 minutes. Cool before serving.

Cinnamon-Almond Pecan Pie

*This is a little different from the
traditional pecan pie and it is a good one!*

⅔ cup sugar	160 ml
1 tablespoon flour	15 ml
2½ teaspoons cinnamon	11 ml
4 eggs, lightly beaten	
1 cup light corn syrup	240 ml
2 tablespoons butter, melted	30 ml
1 tablespoon vanilla	15 ml
1½ teaspoons almond extract	7 ml
1 cup coarsely chopped pecans	240 ml
½ cup slivered almonds	120 ml
1 (9-inch) frozen piecrust	23 cm

- Preheat oven to 400° (204° C).

- In large bowl combine sugar and flour. Add cinnamon, eggs, corn syrup, butter, vanilla and almond extract and mix well.

- Stir in chopped pecans and slivered almonds. Pour filling into piecrust. Cover crust edges with strips of foil to prevent excessive browning.

- Bake for 10 minutes, reduce heat to 325° (162° C) and bake 40 to 45 minutes more or until center of pie is firm.

- Cool completely before serving.

Favorite Chocolate Pie

2 bars unsweetened chocolate, melted
2 (9-inch) frozen piecrusts   2 (23 cm)
1 cup pecan halves   240 ml
1 (3 ounce) package cream cheese, softened   84 g
½ cup (1 stick) butter, melted   120 ml
4 eggs
1½ cups sugar   360 ml
½ cup cocoa   120 ml
1 tablespoon flour   15 ml
1 (12 ounce) can evaporated milk   340 g
¼ cup brandy   60 ml

- Preheat oven to 350° (176° C).

- Spread half melted chocolate on bottom of each piecrust and top evenly with pecans.

- Combine cream cheese, butter and eggs in mixing bowl. Beat until smooth.

- In separate bowl, combine sugar, cocoa, flour and pinch of salt. On low speed, beat into egg mixture and slowly stir in evaporated milk and brandy. Beat another 4 minutes and divide mixture in 2 piecrusts.

- Cover crust edges with strips of foil to prevent excessive browning. Bake for 35 minutes or until center is firm. Cool on wire rack.

Fudgie Brownie Pie

1 (9-inch) frozen piecrust	23 cm
1 (6 ounce) package semi-sweet chocolate chips	168 g
¼ cup (½ stick) butter	60 ml
1 (14 ounce) can sweetened condensed milk	396 g
½ cup biscuit mix	120 ml
2 eggs, slightly beaten	
1 teaspoon vanilla	5 ml
1 cup chopped pecans	240 ml

- Preheat oven to 375° (190° C).

- Bake piecrust for 10 minutes and remove from oven. Reduce heat to 325° (162° C).

- In saucepan over low heat, melt chips in butter and pour into mixing bowl. Add sweetened condensed milk, biscuit mix, eggs and vanilla. Beat until they mix well, add pecans and pour into piecrust.

- Cover crust edges with strips of foil to prevent excessive browning. Bake for 40 minutes or until center is firm. Allow several hours to cool.

BAKE SALE TIP:

Pre-sell your items. Offer to deliver in advance of the sale to offices. Hopefully you can gain additional customers from those who see your great items delivered to their office. Include date, time and location of actual event on tag.

German Chocolate Pie

1 (4 ounce) package German chocolate	114 g
½ cup (1 stick) butter	120 ml
1 (12 ounce) can evaporated milk	340 g
1½ cups sugar	360 ml
3 tablespoons cornstarch	45 ml
2 eggs	
1 teaspoon vanilla	5 ml
1 (9-inch) frozen piecrust	23 cm
⅓ cup flaked coconut	80 ml
½ cup chopped pecans	120 ml

- Preheat oven to 350° (176° C).

- Melt chocolate and butter in saucepan over low heat and gradually blend in milk.

- In mixing bowl mix sugar, cornstarch and pinch of salt thoroughly and beat in eggs and vanilla. Gradually blend into chocolate mixture and pour into piecrust. Combine coconut and pecans and sprinkle over filling.

- Cover crust edges with strips of foil to prevent excessive browning. Bake for 45 to 50 minutes. (Filling will be soft but will set while cooling.) Cool at least 4 hours before slicing.

Kahlua-Pecan Pie

2 tablespoons butter, melted	30 ml
1 cup sugar	240 ml
1 teaspoon vanilla	5 ml
3 tablespoons flour	45 ml
3 eggs	
⅓ cup coffee liqueur	80 ml
½ cup white corn syrup	120 ml
1 cup chopped pecans	240 ml
1 (9-inch) frozen piecrust	23 cm

- Preheat oven to 400° (204° C).

- Melt butter in large bowl, add sugar, vanilla and flour and mix well.

- Add eggs and beat a few minutes by hand. Pour in coffee liqueur and corn syrup and mix.

- Place pecans in piecrust and pour sugar-egg mixture over pecans.

- Cover crust edges with strips of foil to prevent excessive browning.

- Bake for 10 minutes, reduce heat to 325° (162° C) and bake 40 to 45 minutes more or until pie just barely shakes in center.

- Cool completely before serving.

Lemon-Pecan Chess Pie

2¼ cups sugar	540 ml
2 tablespoons flour	30 ml
1 tablespoon cornmeal	15 ml
4 eggs, lightly beaten	
2 tablespoons grated lemon rind	30 ml
¼ cup lemon juice	60 ml
¾ cup chopped pecans	180 ml
1 (9-inch) frozen piecrust	23 cm

- Preheat oven to 400° (204° C).

- Combine sugar, flour and cornmeal in large bowl and toss lightly. Add eggs, lemon rind and lemon juice and mix until smooth. Add pecans to mixture and pour into piecrust.

- Cover crust edges with strips of foil to prevent excessive browning. Bake for 10 minutes. Reduce temperature to 325° (162° C) and bake for 40 to 45 minutes or until center does not shake.

Melt-in-Your-Mouth Cranberry Pie

2 cups fresh or frozen cranberries	480 ml
1½ cups sugar, divided	360 ml
½ cup chopped walnuts or pecans	120 ml
2 eggs	
1 cup flour	240 ml
¼ cup shortening, melted	60 ml
½ cup (1 stick) butter, melted	120 ml

- Preheat oven to 325° (162° C).

- Spray 10-inch (25 cm) deep-dish pie pan and spread cranberries over bottom of pan. Sprinkle with ½ cup (120 ml) sugar and nuts.

- Beat eggs well, add 1 cup (240 ml) sugar gradually and beat thoroughly. Add flour, shortening and butter to sugar mixture and mix well. Pour over top of cranberries and bake for 1 hour or until crust is golden brown.

Mother's Cherry Pie

2 (9-inch) frozen piecrusts	2 (23 cm)
1 cup sugar	240 ml
3 tablespoons cornstarch	45 ml
1 (15 ounce) can cherries with juice	425 g
Red cake coloring	
1 tablespoon butter	15 ml
½ teaspoon almond flavoring	2 ml
1 egg white, beaten	

- Preheat oven to 400° (204° C).

- Line 1 piecrust on 8-inch (20 cm) foil pie pan and trim overhang. Combine sugar, cornstarch and pinch of salt in saucepan and mix well.

- Add cherries and ½ cup (120 ml) juice and cook over medium heat, stirring constantly, until mixture thickens. Add a few drops of red cake coloring.

- Remove from heat and stir in butter and almond flavoring. Let stand about 15 minutes and spoon cherry mixture into piecrust.

- Place second piecrust over top, seal and flute edges with overlapping dough. Spread thin layer of egg white over top of crust with fingers so crust browns nicely.

- Make 3 slits with knife in top crust and bake for 35 minutes or until golden brown and juices begin to bubble. Cool on wire rack.

Mrs. Smith's® Dressed-Up Apple Pie

1 (3 pound) frozen Mrs. Smith's® deep-dish apple pie, thawed	1.3 kg

Praline Topping:

¼ cup (½ stick) butter	60 ml
1¼ cups packed brown sugar	300 ml
⅓ cup whipping cream	80 ml
1 cup powdered sugar	240 ml
1 cup chopped pecans	240 ml

- Preheat oven to 350° (176° C).

- Remove plastic wrap from pie, cut 4 or 5 slits in top of crust and place on baking sheet.

- Bake for 1 hour, remove from oven and shield top of pie with foil. Bake additional 20 minutes, then cool several hours.

- In saucepan, combine butter, brown sugar and whipping cream. Bring to a boil over medium heat and boil for 1 minute.

- Remove from heat and stir in powdered sugar until mixture is smooth. Stir in pecans and mix well.

- Slowly pour praline mixture over pie and spread to cover.

Old-Fashioned Blueberry Pie

4 cups fresh blueberries	1 L
¾ cup sugar	180 ml
¼ cup flour	60 ml
2 tablespoons lemon juice	30 ml
2 (9-inch) frozen piecrusts	2 (23 cm)
2 tablespoons (¼ stick) butter	30 ml

- Preheat oven to 425° (220° C).

- In large bowl, gently mix blueberries and sugar. (If blueberries are tart, add a little more sugar.) Stir in flour and lemon juice. Spoon mixture into pie pan over bottom crust.

- Dot with butter and place top crust over pie filling.

- Fold edges of top crust under edges of bottom crust to seal. Flute edges with fingers and cut several slits in top crust.

- Bake for 15 minutes and remove pie from oven. Cover edges of piecrust with strips of foil to prevent excessive browning.

- Return to oven and bake for 30 to 40 minutes or until pie bubbles and crust is golden brown.

Old-Fashioned Cherry Pie

4 cups pitted cherries	1 L
1¼ cups sugar	300 ml
¼ cup flour	60 ml
¼ teaspoon cinnamon	1 ml
2 (9-inch) frozen piecrusts	2 (23 cm)
2 tablespoons (¼ stick) butter	30 ml

- Preheat oven to 425° (220° C).

- In large bowl, gently mix cherries and sugar. Stir in flour and cinnamon. Spoon mixture over bottom crust in pie pan.

- Dot with butter and place top crust over pie filling.

- Fold edges of top crust under edges of bottom crust to seal. Flute edges with fingers and cut several slits in top crust.

- Bake for 15 minutes and remove pie from oven. Cover edges of piecrust with foil to prevent excessive browning.

- Return to oven and bake for 20 to 25 minutes or until pie bubbles and crust is golden brown.

Pecan Pie Favorite

2 tablespoons flour	30 ml
3 tablespoons butter, melted	45 ml
3 eggs, beaten	
⅔ cup sugar	160 ml
1 cup corn syrup	240 ml
1 teaspoon vanilla	5 ml
1 cup chopped pecans	240 ml
1 (9-inch) frozen piecrust	23 cm

- Preheat oven to 350° (176° C).

- In mixing bowl, combine flour, butter, eggs, sugar, corn syrup and vanilla and mix well. Place pecans in piecrust and pour egg mixture over pecans.

- Bake for 10 minutes, reduce heat to 275° (135° C) and bake for 50 to 55 minutes or until center of pie is fairly firm.

Pecan Pie Variations

Pecan pie recipes have lots of variations. Here are 3 you may enjoy.

1. Substitute 2 tablespoons (30 ml) amaretto for 1 teaspoon (5 ml) vanilla.

2. Add 1 teaspoon (5 ml) cinnamon.

3. Add ½ teaspoon (2 ml) nutmeg.

Pineapple-Coconut Pie

1½ cups sugar	360 ml
3 tablespoons flour	45 ml
3 eggs, well beaten	
2 tablespoons lemon juice	30 ml
1 teaspoon vanilla	5 ml
1 cup flaked coconut	240 ml
1 (8 ounce) can crushed pineapple, drained	227 g
⅓ cup (⅔ stick) butter, melted	80 ml
1 (9-inch) frozen piecrust	23 cm

- Preheat oven to 350° (176° C).

- Combine sugar and flour and stir in eggs, lemon juice and vanilla and mix well. Stir in coconut, pineapple and butter and pour into piecrust.

- Cover crust edges with strips of foil to prevent excessive browning. Bake for 1 hour or until pie is firm in middle.

- If at all possible, make this pie the morning of the bake sale, so the crust doesn't get soggy.

BAKE SALE TIP:

Cut 30-inch (70 cm) square of light yellow plastic wrap and place pie in center. Pull edges up and tie with a pretty colored ribbon and tag telling the name of the pie.

Apricot Pie

2 (15 ounce) cans apricot halves, drained   2 (425 g)
1 (9-inch) frozen piecrust   23 cm
1¼ cups sugar   300 ml
¼ cup flour   60 ml
1 (8 ounce) carton whipping cream, whipped   227 g

- Preheat oven to 325° (162° C).

- Cut each apricot half into 2 pieces and arrange evenly in piecrust.

- Combine sugar and flour and sprinkle over apricots. Pour whipped cream over pie. Cover crust edges with strips of foil to prevent excessive browning. Bake for 1 hour 20 minutes.

Easy Pumpkin Pie

2 eggs
1 (30 ounce) can pumpkin pie mix   900 g
1 (5 ounce) can evaporated milk   143 g
1 (9-inch) frozen deep-dish piecrust   23 cm

- Preheat oven to 400° (204° C).

- Beat eggs lightly in large bowl. Stir in pumpkin pie mix and evaporated milk. Pour into piecrust.

- Cover crust edges with strips of foil to prevent excessive browning.

- Bake for 15 minutes. Reduce temperature to 325° (162° C) and bake 40 more minutes or until knife inserted in center comes out clean. Cool on wire rack.

Thanksgiving Pumpkin Pie

1 (15 ounce) can pumpkin	425 g
1 cup sugar	240 ml
2 eggs, slightly beaten	
1½ teaspoons pumpkin pie spice	7 ml
1 (12 ounce) can evaporated milk	340 g
1 (9-inch) frozen piecrust	23 cm

- Preheat oven to 425° (220° C).

- In bowl, combine pumpkin, sugar, beaten eggs, pumpkin pie spice, evaporated milk and a pinch of salt and mix well.

- Pour into piecrust and bake for 15 minutes. Lower heat to 325° (162° C) and continue baking another 45 to 50 minutes or until knife inserted in center comes out clean.

Old-Fashioned Pecan Pie

3 eggs, beaten	
1 cup sugar	240 ml
1 cup white corn syrup	240 ml
1 cup pecan halves	240 ml
1 teaspoon vanilla extract	5 ml
1 (9-inch) frozen piecrust	23 cm

- Preheat oven to 300° (148° C).

- Beat eggs and sugar until they have lemon color. Add corn syrup, pecans and vanilla and mix well.

- Pour into piecrust. Bake for 1 hour or until center of pie sets.

$Million Dollar⁰⁰ Pie

24 round, buttery crackers, crumbled
1 cup chopped pecans   240 ml
4 egg whites (absolutely no yolks at all)
1 cup sugar   240 ml

- Preheat oven to 350° (176° C).

- In bowl, combine cracker crumbs with pecans.

- In separate mixing bowl, beat egg whites until stiff
  and slowly add sugar while still mixing. Gently fold
  crumbs and pecan mixture into egg whites.

- Pour into pie plate, bake for 20 minutes and cool
  before serving.

Peach-Apricot Pie

1 (15 ounce) can sliced peaches, drained   425 g
1 (15 ounce) can apricots, drained   425 g
1 cup sugar   240 ml
3 tablespoons flour   45 ml
2 (9-inch) frozen piecrusts   2 (23 cm)
2 tablespoons butter   30 ml

- Preheat oven to 400° (204° C).

- In bowl, combine peaches, apricots, sugar and flour
  and mix well. Place fruit in 1 piecrust. Lift second
  piecrust over fruit in bottom piecrust and pinch edges
  together.

- Make several slits in top piecrust and dot with chunks
  of butter. Bake for 45 minutes or until top crust is
  light brown.

Creamy Pecan Pie

1½ cups light corn syrup	360 ml
1 (3 ounce) package instant vanilla pudding	84 g
3 eggs	
2½ tablespoons (⅓ stick) butter, melted	35 ml
2 cups pecan halves	480 ml
1 (9-inch) frozen deep-dish piecrust	23 cm

- Preheat oven to 325° (162° C).

- Combine corn syrup, pudding, eggs and butter, mix well and stir in pecans.

- Pour into deep-dish piecrust. Cover piecrust edges with strips of foil to prevent excessive browning.

- Bake for 35 to 40 minutes or until center of pie is firm.

Cherry Crisp

2 (20 ounce) cans cherry pie filling	2 (567 g)
1 (18 ounce) box white cake mix	510 g
½ cup (1 stick) butter	120 ml
2 cups chopped pecans	480 ml

- Preheat oven to 350° (176° C).

- Pour pie filling into 9 x 13-inch (23 x 33 cm) sprayed baking dish. Sprinkle cake mix over top of filling.

- Dot with butter and cover with pecans.

- Bake uncovered for 45 minutes.

Pecan Tassies

½ cup (1 stick) butter, softened   120 ml
2 (3 ounce) packages cream cheese, softened 2 (84 g)
2 cups flour   480 ml

Filling:

3 eggs, slightly beaten
¼ cup (½ stick) butter, melted   60 ml
2 cups packed brown sugar   480 ml
1 cup chopped pecans   240 ml

- Preheat oven to 375° (190° C).

- Beat butter and cream cheese until smooth. Stir in flour until blended well and chill at least 30 to 45 minutes.

- Divide dough into 24 equal pieces, flatten each into 3-inch (8 cm) round and fit into 24 mini muffin cups. Let dough extend slightly above each cup.

- Combine all filling ingredients and spoon about 1 tablespoon (15 ml) into each cup. Bake for 20 minutes or until pastry is light brown and filling sets.

BAKE SALE TIP:

Before covering a foil platter of pecan tassies with plastic wrap, consider sprinkling a handful of Skittles® around the pecan tassies. That will add a touch of color to your plate of treats!

Easy Apple Turnovers

Filling:

1 (10 ounce) can apple pie filling	280 g
½ cup sugar	120 ml
1 tablespoon lemon juice	15 ml
1 teaspoon cinnamon	5 ml

Crust:

4 - 5 sheets frozen puff pastry, thawed in refrigerator

- Preheat oven to 400° (204° C).

- In food processor, pulse apple pie filling until pieces are half-inch or smaller.

- Unfold 1 sheet puff pastry onto lightly floured work surface and roll into 1 (10-inch/25 cm) square. Cut that square into 4 (5-inch/13 cm) squares.

- Fill each turnover with 2 to 3 tablespoons (30 ml) apple mixture, fold and crimp edges. Repeat cutting squares and use all apple mixture. Place on 1 large foil-lined baking pan.

- Place turnovers in freezer for 15 to 20 minutes. Bake 25 minutes or until turnovers are light brown.

Holiday Fruit Cobbler

Crust:

1¾ cups baking mix	420 ml
¾ cup sugar	180 ml
1 teaspoon cinnamon	5 ml
¼ cup (½ stick) butter, softened	60 ml
1 cup evaporated milk	240 ml

Fruit:

1 (20 ounce) can apple pie filling	567 g
1 cup sweetened dried cranberries	240 ml
½ cup chopped pecans	120 ml

- Preheat oven to 350° (176° C).

- In bowl, combine baking mix, sugar and cinnamon. Cut butter into mixture until crumbly. Stir in evaporated milk and mix well. Pour into 9 x 13-inch (23 x 33 cm) sprayed, floured baking dish.

- In bowl, combine apple pie filling and cranberries, mix well and spread evenly over batter. Sprinkle pecans over fruit and pour ¾ cup (180 ml) hot water over top. Bake for 45 minutes.

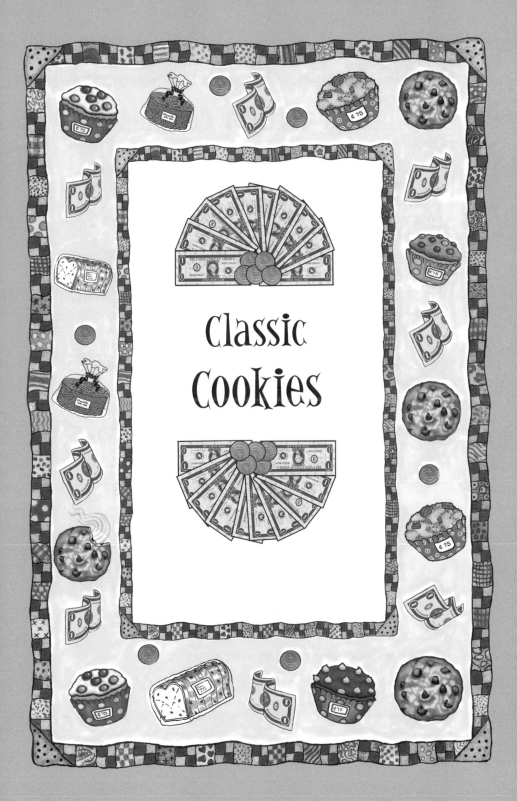

Classic
Cookies

Seven-Layer Cookies

½ cup (1 stick) butter	120 ml
1 cup crushed graham crackers	240 ml
1 (6 ounce) package semi-sweet chocolate chips	168 g
1 (6 ounce) package butterscotch bits	168 g
1 (3.5 ounce) can flaked coconut	100 g
1 (14 ounce) can sweetened condensed milk	396 g
1 cup chopped pecans	240 ml

- Preheat oven to 350° (176° C).

- Melt butter in 9 x 13-inch (23 x 33 cm) baking pan. Sprinkle remaining ingredients in order listed on top of butter.

- Do not stir or mix. Bake for 30 minutes and cool before cutting.

Peanut Butter Cookies

1 cup sugar	240 ml
¾ cup light corn syrup	180 ml
1 (16 ounce) jar crunchy peanut butter	.5 kg
4½ cups chow mein noodles	1.1 L

- In saucepan over medium heat, bring sugar and corn syrup to a boil and stir in peanut butter.

- Remove from heat and stir in noodles.

- Drop by spoonfuls onto wax paper and allow to cool.

Double-Chocolate Cookies

6 egg whites	
3 cups powdered sugar	710 ml
¼ cup cocoa	60 ml
3½ cups finely chopped pecans	830 ml

- Preheat oven to 325° (162° C).

- Beat egg whites until light and frothy. Fold sugar and cocoa into egg whites and beat lightly. Fold in pecans.

- Drop by teaspoonfuls on lightly sprayed, floured cookie sheet.

- Bake for about 20 minutes. Be careful not to over bake. Cool completely before removing from cookie sheet.

Chinese Cookies

1 (6 ounce) package butterscotch chips	168 g
1 (6 ounce) package chocolate chips	168 g
2 cups chow mein noodles	480 ml
1¼ cups salted peanuts	300 ml

- On low heat, melt butterscotch and chocolate chips. Add noodles and peanuts and mix well.

- Drop by teaspoonfuls onto wax paper and refrigerate to harden.

- Store in airtight container.

15-Minute Butterscotch Cookies

1 (18 ounce) box yellow cake mix	510 g
2 eggs, slightly beaten	
½ cup (1 stick) butter, melted	120 ml
⅓ cup packed brown sugar	80 ml
2 teaspoons cocoa powder	10 ml
1 cup butterscotch chips	240 ml
¾ cup chopped pecans	180 ml

- Preheat oven to 350° (176° C).

- Combine cake mix, eggs, butter, brown sugar and cocoa powder in large bowl; stir to blend well.

- Stir in butterscotch chips and pecans and drop by tablespoonfuls onto foil-lined baking sheet. Bake for 14 minutes and cool cookies completely on wire rack before stacking.

Butterfinger Cookies

½ cup (1 stick) butter, softened	120 ml
¾ cup sugar	180 ml
¾ cup packed brown sugar	180 ml
2 egg whites	
1½ teaspoons vanilla	7 ml
1 cup flour	240 ml
½ teaspoon baking soda	2 ml
1¼ cups chunky peanut butter	300 ml
6 mini Butterfinger® candy bars	

- Preheat oven to 350° (176° C).

- Combine butter and both sugars in large bowl. Add egg whites and mix well.

- Stir in vanilla, flour, baking soda, pinch of salt and peanut butter and mix gently. Chop candy bars into coarse chunks and add to cookie mixture with spoon.

- Drop tablespoonfuls on sprayed cookie sheet and bake for 16 minutes or until edges are golden brown. (Watch closely because you may need to rotate cookie sheet for cookies to bake evenly.)

Choc-O-Cherry Cookies

A chocolate lover's dream!

½ cup (1 stick) butter, softened	120 ml
1 cup sugar	240 ml
1 egg	
½ teaspoon vanilla	2 ml
1½ cups flour	360 ml
½ cup cocoa	120 ml
¼ teaspoon baking powder	1 ml
¼ teaspoon baking soda	1 ml
1 (10 ounce) jar maraschino cherries, drained	280 g
1 (6 ounce) package chocolate chips	168 g

- Preheat oven to 350° (176° C).

- Cream butter, sugar, egg and vanilla until light and fluffy. Add dry ingredients with ¼ teaspoon (1 ml) salt and mix.

- Cut cherries in quarters, add cherries and chocolate chips and mix.

- Drop by teaspoonfuls onto cookie sheet and bake for 15 minutes.

Chocolate-Oatmeal Cookies

1 ¾ cups old-fashioned oats, divided	420 ml
1 cup flour	240 ml
¾ teaspoon baking powder	4 ml
½ teaspoon baking soda	2 ml
1 cup (2 sticks) butter, softened	240 ml
1 ¼ cups packed light brown sugar	300 ml
1 large egg, slightly beaten	
1 teaspoon vanilla	5 ml
3 (1 ounce) bars milk chocolate, melted, cooled	3 (28 g)
1 cup semi-sweet chocolate chips	240 ml
1 cup chopped pecans	240 ml

- Preheat oven to 350° (176° C).

- Place 1 cup (240 ml) oats in food processor and grind to fine crumbs. Transfer to large bowl and add flour, baking powder, baking soda and ½ teaspoon (2 ml) salt.

- With mixer, beat butter and brown sugar. Add egg and vanilla and beat until they blend well. Add melted chocolate and beat until they mix well. Stir in remaining oats and flour mixture and beat about 15 seconds.

- Stir in chocolate chips and pecans and roll about 2 tablespoons (30 ml) mixture into balls.

- Place 2 inches (5 cm) apart on cookie sheet and bake for 15 to 17 minutes or until cookies crack on top. Store in airtight containers.

Christmas Cookies

1 cup (2 sticks) butter, softened	240 ml
¾ cup sugar	180 ml
1 cup packed brown sugar	240 ml
1 teaspoon vanilla	5 ml
2 eggs	
2½ cups flour	600 ml
1 teaspoon baking soda	5 ml
1 (12 ounce) package white chocolate chips	340 g
1 cup chopped pecans	240 ml
1 (3.5 ounce) can flaked coconut	100 g
20 red candied cherries, chopped	
20 green candied cherries, chopped	

- Preheat oven to 350° (176° C).

- In mixing bowl, cream butter, sugars, vanilla and eggs and beat well.

- Add flour, baking soda and ½ teaspoon (2 ml) salt and mix well. Stir in chocolate chips, pecans, coconut and cherries.

- Drop dough by teaspoonfuls onto cookie sheet. (Dough will be very stiff.)

- Bake for 8 to 10 minutes. Cool before storing.

Drop Cookies

1 cup (2 sticks) butter, softened	240 ml
¾ cup cornstarch	180 ml
⅓ cup powdered sugar	80 ml
1 cup flour	

Icing:

1 (3 ounce) package cream cheese, softened	84 g
1 teaspoon vanilla	5 ml
1 cup powdered sugar	240 ml

- Preheat oven to 350° (176° C).

- Mix butter, cornstarch, sugar and flour and mix well.

- Drop on cookie sheet in small balls and flatten slightly.

- Bake for about 15 minutes but do not brown.

- With mixer, blend icing ingredients and mix well. Ice cool cookies.

BAKE SALE TIP:

For a nice touch, sprinkle a few vanilla-yogurt raisins over top of icing. They are delicious.

Frost-Bite Cookies

1 (18 ounce) package devil's food cake mix	510 g
½ cup oil	120 ml
2 eggs	
1 cup white chocolate chips	240 ml
1 tablespoon oil	15 ml

- Preheat oven to 350° (176° C).

- Combine cake mix, oil and eggs in bowl and mix well.

- Drop by teaspoons onto non-stick cookie sheet.

- Bake for 10 to 12 minutes. Cool and remove to wire rack.

- Microwave white chocolate and oil in small, deep bowl for 2 to 3 minutes on LOW power and stir once. Let stand 2 minutes and stir until smooth.

- Dip one-third of each cookie in white chocolate and place on wax paper-lined baking sheets. Chill until white chocolate is firm.

Holiday Spritz Cookies

¾ cup (1¼ sticks) butter, softened	180 ml
1¼ cups sugar	300 ml
1 egg, well beaten	
1 teaspoon almond flavoring	5 ml
3 cups flour	710 ml
1 teaspoon baking powder	5 ml

- Preheat oven to 350° (176° C).

- Cream butter and sugar with mixer, add beaten egg and almond flavoring and beat well.

- Stir in flour and baking powder into creamed mixture.

- Place dough in cookie press and press out desired shapes onto baking sheets.

- Bake for about 8 minutes or until light brown.

BAKE SALE TIP:

Use decorating icings or sprinkles found in the grocery store to decorate cookies or add a little food coloring to batter for a holiday touch.

Holly-Almond Cookies

1 cup (2 sticks) butter, softened	240 ml
1 (3 ounce) package cream cheese, softened	84 g
1½ cups powdered sugar	360 ml
2 cups flour	480 ml
1 cup finely chopped almonds	240 ml
2 teaspoons almond flavoring	10 ml
1 teaspoon vanilla	5 ml
½ pound whole candied cherries	227 g

- Preheat oven to 325° (162° C).

- Beat butter, cream cheese and sugar, add flour and mix well.

- Stir in almonds, almond flavoring and vanilla and mix well.

- Take spoonful of dough and form ball with your hands. Push candied cherry in center of each ball (not to cover cherry, just to flatten cookie slightly).

- Bake for 20 to 25 minutes or until edges are barely brown.

Irresistible Peanut Butter Cookies

1 (18 ounce) package refrigerated peanut butter cookie dough	510 g
1 cup rice crispy cereal, divided	240 ml
1 (16 ounce) package M&M's® candies, divided	.5 kg
1 (18 ounce) package refrigerated sugar cookie dough	510 g
1½ cups finely chopped roasted peanuts	360 ml

- Preheat oven to 350° (176° C).

- In large bowl, combine peanut butter cookie dough, ½ cup (120 ml) cereal and 1 cup (240 ml) candies and mix until they blend well.

- In another bowl, combine sugar cookie dough, ½ cup cereal and 1 cup (240 ml) candies and mix. Combine half peanut butter dough with half sugar cookie dough by folding together just enough to marble. Repeat with remaining dough.

- Take 1 heaping tablespoon (15 ml) dough and form into 1½-inch (3 cm) balls. Place chopped peanuts in bowl, dip 1 side of balls into peanuts and place on sprayed cookie sheet, peanut side up. With fork, mash down slightly on cookie, but keep chopped peanuts securely on cookie. Bake for 12 to 14 minutes and cool.

BAKE SALE TIP:

With colored M&M's® showing up on top of the cookies, these cookies will sell themselves. Place cookies, overlapping one another, on a gold doily-lined plastic plate. Cover with clear plastic wrap so cookies are clearly visible.

Jingle Bell Cookies

These are almost like candy!

1 cup sugar	240 ml
½ cup (1 stick) butter	120 ml
½ cup evaporated milk	120 ml
1½ cups mini marshmallows	360 ml
1½ cups graham cracker crumbs or	
vanilla wafers	360 ml
1 cup chopped pecans	240 ml

- Combine sugar, butter and evaporated milk in saucepan. Boil for 6 minutes and stir constantly.

- Remove from heat, add marshmallows and stir until marshmallows melt.

- Stir in graham cracker crumbs and pecans. Hand beat until slightly cool and mixture becomes fairly stiff.

- Quickly drop by tablespoonfuls onto buttered wax paper to cool. Store in covered container.

BAKE SALE TIP:

These cookies are really pretty on a red plastic plate. Buy some inexpensive plastic red and green holly, Christmas trinkets, tiny poinsettias, etc. Any little Christmas items will really dress up this plate of cookies.

Lollipop Cookies

1 (18 ounce) box carrot cake mix	510 g
⅓ cup oil	80 ml
3 eggs	
2 tablespoons flour	30 ml
24 popsicle sticks	
1 (16 ounce) carton caramel icing	.5 kg
Squeezable colored cake icings	

- Preheat oven to 375° (190° C).

- Prepare cake according to package directions using ¾ cup (180 ml) water, oil, eggs and flour and mix well. Drop dough by rounded tablespoonfuls about 3 inches (8 cm) apart onto cookie sheet. Insert wooden sticks in edge (horizontally) of dough until tip is in center.

- Bake for 10 minutes or until puffed and there is almost no indentation when touched; cool 1 minute. Remove from cookie sheet carefully so stick stays in place. Place on another baking sheet lined with wax paper. Cool completely.

- Spread with caramel icing and squeeze tubes of colored icing to draw "tick, tack, toe" game, smiling faces, et cetera over caramel icing. Let set at least 1 or 2 hours.

BAKE SALE TIP:

Wrap each cookie with colorful plastic wrap and tie a ribbon on the stick.

Macadamia Nut Cookies

These are just like those cookies you buy at the mall.

½ cup shortening	120 ml
½ cup (1 stick) butter, softened	120 ml
2½ cups flour, divided	600 ml
1 cup packed brown sugar	240 ml
½ cup sugar	120 ml
2 eggs	
1 teaspoon vanilla	5 ml
½ teaspoon butter flavoring	2 ml
½ teaspoon baking soda	2 ml
2 cups white chocolate chips	480 ml
1 (3.5 ounce) jar macadamia nuts, chopped	100 g

- Preheat oven to 350° (176° C).

- In mixing bowl, beat shortening and butter. Add half of flour and mix well.

- Add both sugars, eggs, vanilla, butter flavoring and baking soda and beat until mixture mixes well.

- Add remaining flour, mix well and stir in white chocolate chips and nuts.

- Drop dough by teaspoonfuls onto cookie sheet. Bake for about 8 minutes. Cool completely before packaging.

Mincemeat Cookies

For you "Gen-X'ers" who don't know how good mincemeat is, check it out – it's great!

1 cup (2 sticks) butter, softened	240 ml
1⅔ cups sugar	400 ml
1 teaspoon baking soda	5 ml
3 eggs, beaten	
3¼ cups flour	770 ml
1¼ cups chopped pecans	300 ml
1 cup prepared mincemeat	240 ml

- Preheat oven to 350° (176° C).

- Cream butter and add sugar gradually.

- Dissolve baking soda in 2 teaspoons (10 ml) hot water. Pour into butter mixture, add egg and mix.

- Add ½ teaspoon (2 ml) salt and flour to creamed mixture and mix well. Add pecans and mincemeat.

- Drop by teaspoonfuls on sprayed cookie sheet.

- Bake for 14 to 15 minutes or until cookies begin to brown.

BAKE SALE TIP:

Dress up the cookies by dipping one edge of a cookie in melted white or dark chocolate or frost with decorations for the season or any special occasion.

Old-Fashioned Peach Cookies

1 (20 ounce) can peach pie filling	567 g
1 (18 ounce) box yellow cake mix	510 g
2 eggs	
1 cup finely chopped pecans	240 ml
Sugar	

- Preheat oven to 350° (176° C).

- In blender, process pie filling until smooth.

- In large bowl, combine pie filling, dry cake mix and eggs and blend well. Stir in pecans.

- Drop by tablespoonfuls onto sprayed cookie sheet. Sprinkle with sugar.

- Bake for 15 minutes or until cookies are light brown around edges.

BAKE SALE TIP:

Decorate your plate of cookies with a hand full of Smoothie Mix Skittles® sprinkled on top. The light colors of the Skittles® will be pretty with the cookies. A pretty pink bow in the middle of the plastic wrap make packages very appealing as well.

Ritz® Cracker Cookies

1 (14 ounce) can sweetened condensed milk	396 g
1 cup chopped dates	240 ml
½ cup chopped pecans	120 ml
Ritz® crackers	
1 (3 ounce) package cream cheese	84 g
2½ cups powdered sugar	600 ml
1 teaspoon vanilla	5 ml
2 - 3 tablespoons cream	30 ml

• Preheat oven to 350° (176° C).

• Combine sweetened condensed milk and dates in saucepan and cook, stirring constantly, until mixture thickens. Stir in pecans and spoon mixture on Ritz® crackers. Bake for 6 minutes.

• Beat cream cheese, powdered sugar, vanilla and 2 tablespoons (30 ml) cream. Add more cream if needed for spreading consistency. Frost each cookie and store in airtight container.

Speedy Chocolate Cookies

1½ cups sugar	360 ml
½ cup (1 stick) butter	120 ml
½ cup milk	120 ml
½ cup cocoa	120 ml
1 teaspoon vanilla	5 ml
3½ cups oats	830 ml
½ cup flaked coconut	120 ml
¾ cup chopped pecans	180 ml

- Combine sugar, butter, milk and cocoa in saucepan over medium heat. Cook, stirring constantly, until mixture begins to boil. Remove from heat and stir in vanilla, oats, coconut and pecans.

- Work quickly and drop tablespoonfuls of mixture onto buttered or sprayed wax paper. Let stand at room temperature to cool before storing in airtight containers.

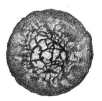

Super Fudge Cookies

1 (18 ounce) box devil's food cake mix	510 g
½ cup (1 stick) butter, softened	120 ml
1 large egg	
1 cup finely chopped pecans	240 ml
1 (12 ounce) package Milky Way PoPables®	

- Preheat oven to 350° (176° C).

- Combine cake mix and butter and mix until crumbly. Stir in egg and 2 tablespoons (30 ml) water and blend until smooth. Fold in pecans and mix well.

- Shape dough into 1-inch (2.5 cm) balls and place 2 inches (5 cm) apart on sprayed cookie sheet. Bake for 8 to 10 minutes. When done, immediately place 1 candy in center of each cookie and cool.

BAKE SALE TIP:

Place these rich chocolate cookies on an inexpensive 9 x 13-inch (23 x 33 cm) plastic plate. You can even buy paper dollies in 9 x 13-inch (23 x 33 cm) shapes. Just to "fancy up" the plate, scatter some colorful M&M's® around edges of cookies. Color and chocolate always add interest for the big sale.

Sweet-Salty Drop Cookies

1 cup (2 sticks) butter, softened	240 ml
1 cup packed light brown sugar	240 ml
⅔ cup sugar	160 ml
2 eggs, slightly beaten	
2 teaspoons vanilla	10 ml
2½ cups flour	600 ml
¾ teaspoon baking powder	4 ml
2 cups broken-up pretzel sticks	480 ml
1 cup honey-roasted chopped peanuts	240 ml
1½ cups semi-sweet chocolate chips	360 ml

- Preheat oven to 350° (176° C).

- Cream butter, both sugars in large mixing bowl. Add eggs, one at a time, and vanilla and beat well after each addition.

- Stir flour and baking powder into creamed mixture. Stir in pretzel sticks, peanuts and chocolate chips.

- Drop by heaping tablespoonfuls 2 inches (5 cm) apart onto cookie sheet and bake for about 12 minutes or until edges are light brown. Cool on wire racks.

Vanishing Butter Cookies

1 (18 ounce) box butter cake mix	510 g
1 (3.4 ounce) package butterscotch instant pudding mix	100 g
1 cup oil	240 ml
1 egg, beaten	
1¼ cups chopped pecans	300 ml

- Preheat oven to 350° (176° C).

- Mix cake and pudding mixes by hand and stir in oil. Add egg, mix thoroughly and stir in pecans.

- Place dough on cookie sheet by teaspoonfuls about 2 inches (5 cm) apart.

- Bake for 8 or 9 minutes. Do not overcook.

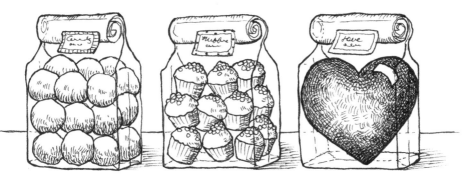

White Chocolate-Almond Cookies

¾ cup firmly packed light brown sugar	180 ml
½ cup sugar	120 ml
½ cup (1 stick) butter, softened	120 ml
½ cup shortening	120 ml
1½ teaspoons vanilla	7 ml
1 egg	
1¾ cups plus 2 tablespoons flour	420 ml/30 ml
1 teaspoon baking soda	5 ml
1 cup white chocolate chips	240 ml
⅓ cup slivered almonds	80 ml

- Preheat oven to 350° (176° C).

- In large bowl, combine both sugars, butter, shortening, vanilla and egg and mix well.

- Stir in flour, baking soda and ½ teaspoon (2 ml) salt and blend well. Stir in white chocolate chips and almonds and mix well. (Batter will be stiff.)

- Drop by teaspoonfuls on cookie sheet and bake for 10 minutes or until cookies are light, golden brown.

- Store cookies in sealed container.

Yummy Cookies

3 egg whites
1¼ cups sugar   300 ml
2 teaspoons vanilla extract   10 ml
3½ cups frosted corn flakes   830 ml
1 cup chopped pecans   240 ml

- Preheat oven to 250° (121° C).

- Beat egg whites until stiff and gradually add sugar and vanilla.

- Fold in frosted corn flakes and pecans and drop by teaspoonfuls on cookie sheet.

- Bake for 40 minutes.

BAKE SALE TIP:

It would look really great to sprinkle vanilla-yogurt raisins around the outside edge of your plate. One (8 ounce/227 g) package will be enough for 2 or 3 plates of cookies and adds interest for the big sale.

Goody
Bag

Cookie Sticks

Here are three different cookie presentations for bake sales. They are also so easy and very cute! Buyers can't resist them.

Sugar Cookie Sticks*

1 (18 ounce) package refrigerated Nestle® sugar cookie dough	510 g
20 popsicle sticks	
1 (16 ounce) carton confetti icing	.5 kg
1 (7 ounce) package tropical trio fruits	198 g

- Preheat oven to 325° (162° C).

- This cookie dough is ready to bake. Just break along prescored lines and place on cookie sheet 2 inches (5 cm) apart. Leave enough space to place popsicle stick through middle (horizontally) of cookie.

- Bake 16 to 18 minutes. Cool, spread confetti icing over cookies and sprinkle top with 1 tablespoon (15 ml) tropical fruits.

DECORATING TIPS: These cookies are special treats at kids' parties. Kids love to decorate their own cookie sticks. They can write their names on cookies with colored icings in tubes found in the grocery store. Use your imagination!!

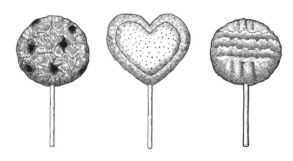

Peanut Butter Cookie Sticks*

1 (18 ounce) package refrigerated Nestle® peanut butter cookie dough	510 g
20 popsicle sticks	
1 (16 ounce) carton caramel icing	.5 kg
1 16 ounce) package Reese's® peanut butter candy in shell	.5 kg

• Use directions for Cookie Sticks on page 160.

Chocolate Cookie Sticks*

1 (18 ounce) package refrigerated Nestle® chocolate cookie dough	510 g
20 popsicle sticks	
1 (16 ounce) can coconut-pecan icing	.5 kg
1 (10 ounce) package Nestle® swirled dark and white chocolate chips	280 g

• Use directions for Cookie Sticks on page 160.

BAKE SALE TIP:

The best way to display the cookie sticks is to place a sheet of styrofoam on table and push the sticks down in the styrofoam. These can be sold individually so each child can pick.

When you make the cookies with the popsicle sticks, cover the cookie part with a colorful cellophane wrap and tie with a ribbon.

Christmas Cookie Cut-Outs

6 tablespoons butter, softened	90 ml
1 cup sugar	240 ml
2 eggs	
1 teaspoon vanilla	5 ml
2½ cups flour	600 ml
1 teaspoon baking powder	5 ml
Powdered sugar	

- Preheat oven to 375° (190° C).

- In large mixing bowl, combine butter, sugar, eggs and vanilla, beat until they blend well and are light and fluffy.

- Add flour, baking powder and 1 teaspoon (5 ml) salt. Beat until all ingredients mix well.

- Cover and chill dough in refrigerator for 1 hour.

- Sprinkle powdered sugar on counter. (Cookies will not toughen when rolled in powdered sugar.) Roll dough ⅛-inch (.4 cm) thick and cut into desired shapes.

- Bake for 6 to 8 minutes. Remove immediately from cookie sheet and cool before decorating.

BAKE SALE TIP:

There is a wide variety of decorating icings available at grocery stores. Many are in tubes so that even the smallest children can quickly become artists. Use your imagination!

Coconut Yummies

1 (12 ounce) package white chocolate chips   340 g
¼ cup (½ stick) butter   60 ml
16 large marshmallows
2 cups quick-cooking oats   480 ml
1 cup flaked coconut   240 ml

- In saucepan over low heat, melt chocolate chips, butter and marshmallows and stir until smooth.

- Stir in oats and coconut and mix well. Drop by rounded teaspoonfuls onto wax paper-lined baking sheets. Chill until set and store in airtight container.

Peanut Butter Balls

¾ cup light corn syrup   180 ml
2½ cups extra crunchy peanut butter   600 ml
2¼ cups graham cracker crumbs   540 ml
1¼ cups powdered sugar   300 ml
1 (12 ounce) jar chocolate ice cream topping   340 g

- Combine corn syrup, peanut butter, graham cracker crumbs and powdered sugar in large bowl and mix until smooth. Shape into 1-inch (2.5 cm) balls and place on baking sheet with paper lined wax paper. Chill for at least 30 minutes.

BAKE SALE TIP:

You could sell this with chocolate ice cream topping and toothpicks for dipping or just put the recipe on a card with the suggestion of "dipping" in chocolate.

Goody Bag

Holiday Fruit Balls

1½ pounds candied cherries	.7 kg
½ pound candied pineapple	227 g
1 (8 ounce) box pitted chopped dates	227 g
1 (7 ounce) can flaked coconut	198 g
4 cups chopped pecans	1 L
1 (14 ounce) can sweetened condensed milk	396 g

- Preheat oven to 350° (176° C).

- Chop cherries, pineapple and dates and mix well by hand.

- Add coconut and pecans, pour sweetened condensed milk over mixture and mix well.

- Put 1 teaspoon (5 ml) mixture in miniature paper cups and place on cookie sheet.

- Bake for 20 to 25 minutes and store in covered container. Makes 150 to 200 fruit balls.

  TIP: These will keep in refrigerator for months if you can keep the family from eating them! My friend says it is not Christmas unless she makes these!

Sugar-Almond No-Bake Balls

2 cups finely crushed, crispy unfrosted	
sugar cookies	480 ml
1 cup finely chopped almonds, toasted	240 ml
1½ cups powdered sugar, divided	360 ml
¼ cup light corn syrup	60 ml
2 tablespoons almond or orange liqueur	30 ml
2 tablespoons butter, softened	30 ml

- Combine crushed cookies, almonds, 1 cup (240 ml) powdered sugar, corn syrup, liqueur and butter in mixing bowl. Stir with wooden spoon until they mix well.

- Shape into 1-inch (2.5 cm) balls and roll balls in remaining ½ cup (120 ml) powdered sugar.

- Let stand at least 2 hours and roll balls again in powdered sugar.

BAKE SALE TIP:

Place balls on 10 to 12-inch (25 cm) plastic plate with silver paper doilies. Do not stack.

Dreamy Date Balls

½ cup (1 stick) butter	120 ml
1 cup sugar	240 ml
1 (8 ounce) box chopped dates	227 g
1 cup rice crispy cereal	240 ml
1 cup chopped pecans	240 ml
1 teaspoon vanilla	5 ml
Powdered sugar	

- In large saucepan, combine butter, sugar and chopped dates. Cook on medium heat, stirring constantly, until all ingredients melt and blend well.

- Remove from heat, add rice cereal, chopped pecans and vanilla and stir to mix well.

- Roll into balls about ¾ inches (1.8 cm) in diameter.

- Drop balls, a few at a time, into small grocery sack or plastic bag with enough powdered sugar to cover.

- Shake lightly until date balls coat with sugar. Store in airtight container.

    TIP: These may be frozen.

Cherry-Pecan Slices

A cherry lover's delight!

2 cups powdered sugar	480 ml
1 cup (2 sticks) butter, softened	240 ml
1 egg	
2 tablespoons milk	30 ml
1 teaspoon vanilla	5 ml
2¼ cups flour	540 ml
2 cups whole candied red cherries	480 ml
1 cup chopped pecans	240 ml

- In mixing bowl, cream sugar and butter until slightly fluffy. Add egg, milk and vanilla, mix and beat in flour. Batter will be stiff.

- Stir in cherries and pecans and mix well. Chill dough 1 hour.

- Sprinkle tiny bit of flour on wax paper. Shape dough into 2 (10-inch/25 cm) rolls and wrap in wax paper. Chill at least 3 hours or overnight.

- Preheat oven to 375° (190° C).

- Cut rolls into ¼-inch (.6 cm) slices. Place on cookie sheets.

- Bake for 10 to 12 minutes. Check cookies in 10 minutes; edges should be slightly brown. Cool on wire racks and store in covered container.

Butterscotch Delights

2 cups flour	480 ml
1 cup packed brown sugar	240 ml
1 teaspoon baking powder	5 ml
½ teaspoon baking soda	2 ml
1 teaspoon ground cinnamon	5 ml
2 eggs, lightly beaten	
⅔ cup oil	160 ml
1 teaspoon vanilla	5 ml
1¼ cups butterscotch chips	300 ml

- Preheat oven to 400° (204° C).

- Combine flour, brown sugar, baking powder, baking soda and cinnamon in large bowl. Stir in eggs, oil and vanilla and mix well. Add butterscotch chips and mix thoroughly.

- Roll 1 tablespoon (15 ml) dough into ball and place balls 3 inches (8 cm) apart on cookie sheet.

- Bake for 7 to 8 minutes. Cool about 5 minutes on baking sheet and transfer to cooling rack.

Snappy Oats

3 cups quick-rolled oats	710 ml
1 cup chocolate chips	240 ml
½ cup flaked coconut	120 ml
½ cup chopped pecans	120 ml
2 cups sugar	480 ml
¾ cup (1½ sticks) butter	180 ml
½ cup evaporated milk	120 ml

- Combine oats, chocolate chips, coconut and pecans in large bowl. In saucepan, boil sugar, butter and milk for 1 to 2 minutes and stir constantly.

- Pour hot mixture over oat-chocolate mixture in bowl and stir until chocolate chips melt. Drop by teaspoonfuls on wax paper. Cool at room temperature and store in covered container.

   TIP: Use white chocolate chips and ¾ cup (180 ml) candied, sliced cherries for a colorful variation.

BAKE SALE TIP:

Schedule a bake day to prepare for a special event – for school, church, special organization, etc. Decorate the whole bake sale area with appropriate holiday colors and have volunteers dress the part.

Goody Bag

Nutty Sandies

1 cup (2 sticks) butter, softened	240 ml
⅔ cup sugar	160 ml
2 cups flour	480 ml
1 tablespoon vanilla	15 ml
2 cups finely chopped pecans, divided	480 ml
1 (13 ounce) bag Snickers® minis	370 g

- Preheat oven to 350° (176° C).

- In large bowl, combine butter and sugar and beat until fluffy. Add flour, ¼ teaspoon (1 ml) salt, vanilla and half chopped pecans and mix well until dough forms. Shape dough into 2 (12-inch/32 cm) logs.

- Place remaining pecans on wax paper and roll each log over pecans until they cover completely. Wrap each log in plastic wrap and refrigerate 1 hour.

- Cut logs into 24 slices each about ½-thick (1.2 cm). Place slices about 1-inch (2.4 cm) apart on sprayed cookie sheets. Bake for 15 to 20 minutes or until golden.

- While cookies are baking, cut several Snickers® minis in half. Remove cookies from oven and immediately press half mini in center of each cookie. Cool completely before serving.

BAKE SALE TIP:

For bake sale, place cookies on plastic platters lined with paper doilies. Cover with plastic wrap and tuck edges down securely.

Ginger Snaps

¾ cup shortening	180 ml
1¼ cups sugar, divided	300 ml
1 egg	
2 cups flour	480 ml
2 teaspoons baking soda	10 ml
2 teaspoons cinnamon	10 ml
1 teaspoon ground cloves	5 ml
1 teaspoon ground ginger	5 ml
4 tablespoons molasses	60 ml

- Preheat oven to 375° (190° C).

- Cream shortening and 1 cup (240 ml) sugar, add egg and beat well. Stir in dry ingredients and molasses and mix well. Roll in small balls and roll in remaining sugar.

- Place on cookie sheet and bake for about 8 minutes. Cool before storing.

BAKE SALE TIP:

Make bake sale items irresistible!! Keep the wrapping simple, yet festive. Don't overpower the delicious items inside.

Whippersnappers

¾ cup packed brown sugar	180 ml
¾ cup white sugar	180 ml
1½ cups shortening	360 ml
2 large eggs	
1½ cups flour	360 ml
½ teaspoon baking soda	2 ml
2¾ cups oats	660 ml
½ cup chopped pecans	120 ml
½ cup peanut butter	120 ml
1½ teaspoons vanilla	7 ml
1 (6 ounce) package chocolate chips	168 g

- Preheat oven to 350° (176° C).

- In bowl, cream both sugars and shortening. Add eggs and beat well.

- Sift flour, baking soda and ½ teaspoon (2 ml) salt and add to cream mixture. Stir in oats, pecans, peanut butter, vanilla and chocolate chips.

- Drop by teaspoonfuls on cookie sheet and bake for 12 to 14 minutes or until cookies brown on edge.

Gum Drop Chews

1 cup flour	240 ml
½ teaspoon baking powder	2 ml
½ teaspoon baking soda	2 ml
1 egg	
½ cup packed brown sugar	120 ml
½ cup sugar	120 ml
½ cup (1 stick) butter, softened	120 ml
1 teaspoon vanilla	5 ml
2 cups gumdrops, cut up	480 ml
1 cup oats	240 ml
1 cup chopped pecans	240 ml

- Preheat oven to 350° (176° C).

- In mixing bowl, combine flour, baking powder, baking soda and ⅛ teaspoon (.5 ml) salt.

- Add egg, both sugars, butter and vanilla and mix well with dry ingredients.

- Add gumdrops, oats and pecans and mix. Drop by teaspoonfuls on cookie sheet. Bake for 12 to 15 minutes.

   TIP: For a variation, use orange slices in place of gumdrops.

Coconut-Chocolate Drops

1 cup sweetened condensed milk	240 ml
4 cups flaked coconut	1 L
2/3 cup miniature semi-sweet chocolate bits	160 ml
1 teaspoon vanilla extract	5 ml
1/2 teaspoon almond extract	2 ml

- Preheat oven to 325° (162° C).

- Stir sweetened condensed milk and coconut together to form a gooey mixture. Add chocolate bits, vanilla and almond and stir until they blend well. Drop by teaspoonfuls onto sprayed baking sheet. Bake for 12 minutes.

No-Bake Chocolate Drops

1 (6 ounce) package semi-sweet chocolate chips	168 g
1/2 cup extra crunchy peanut butter	120 ml
1 (5 ounce) package chow mein noodles	143 g
1 cup salted, honey-roasted peanuts	240 ml

- Combine baking chips and peanut butter in saucepan on low heat and stir constantly until chocolate chips melt.

- Add noodles and peanuts and stir until ingredients coat evenly with chocolate. Drop by heaping teaspoonfuls onto wax paper and chill several hours. Store at room temperature.

Coconut Macaroons

2 (7 ounce) packages flaked coconut   2 (198 g)
1 (14 ounce) can sweetened condensed milk 396 g
2 teaspoons vanilla   10 ml
½ teaspoon almond extract   2 ml

- Preheat oven to 350° (176° C). In mixing bowl, combine coconut, sweetened condensed milk, vanilla and almond extract and mix well.

- Drop by rounded teaspoonfuls onto foil-lined cookie sheet.

- Bake for 8 to 10 minutes or until light brown around edges. Immediately remove from foil. (Macaroons will stick if allowed to cool on foil.) Store at room temperature.

Lemon-Coconut Macaroons

⅔ cup sweetened condensed milk   160 ml
1 large egg white
2 teaspoons lemon juice   10 ml
1 teaspoon lemon zest   5 ml
3½ cups flaked coconut   830 ml

- Preheat oven to 325° (162° C). Mix sweetened condensed milk, egg white, lemon juice and lemon zest and stir in coconut. Drop by teaspoonfuls, 2 inches (5 cm) apart, on cookie sheet covered with parchment paper or foil.

- Bake for 20 minutes or until light brown. Cool completely and carefully remove from parchment paper or foil.

Bird's Nests

1 (16 ounce) box shredded wheat, crushed   .5 kg
1 cup peanut butter   240 ml
1 (12 ounce) package milk chocolate chips,
   melted   340 g
Jelly beans

- Combine and mix crushed wheat, peanut butter and chocolate chips and mix well. Shape into nests on foil or place in small muffin pans and press into nests.

- Let stand several hours and place 3 jelly beans in nest or other small shaped candies to go with season of the year.

BAKE SALE TIP:

Make sure everyone can see these great little bird's nests. Place them on a plastic tray lined with a gold paper doily and cover with plastic wrap.

Peanut Krispies

½ cup (1 stick) butter   120 ml
2 cups peanut butter   480 ml
1 (16 ounce) box powdered sugar   .5 kg
3½ cups rice crispy cereal   830 ml
¾ cup chopped peanuts   180 ml

- Melt butter in large saucepan. Add peanut butter and mix well.

- Add powdered sugar, cereal and peanuts and mix.

- Drop by teaspoonfuls onto wax paper.

Easy Sand Tarts

1 cup (2 sticks) butter, softened	240 ml
¾ cup powdered sugar	180 ml
2 cups sifted flour	480 ml
1 cup chopped pecans	240 ml
1 teaspoon vanilla extract	5 ml

- Preheat oven to 325° (162° C).

- In mixing bowl, cream butter and powdered sugar. Slowly add flour, pecans and vanilla.

- Roll into crescent shape and place on baking sheet. Bake for 20 minutes.

- Roll in extra powdered sugar after tarts cool.

No-Bake Crunchy Clusters

½ cup (1 stick) butter   120 ml
1 (12 ounce) package peanut butter chips   340 g
4 cups corn flakes   1 L
1 (16 ounce) package Snickers® minis,
  chopped   .5 kg

- Place butter and peanut butter chips in heavy saucepan over medium-low heat. Cook, stirring constantly, until peanut butter chips melt and mixture is smooth.

- Stir in corn flakes and Snickers® pieces. Drop into mounds on cookie sheet lined with wax paper. Let stand about 1 hour.

Peanut Butter Gems

1 cup shortening	240 ml
1 cup creamy peanut butter	240 ml
1 cup sugar	240 ml
1 cup powdered sugar	240 ml
2 eggs, slightly beaten	
1 teaspoon vanilla	5 ml
2 cups flour	480 ml
2 teaspoons baking soda	10 ml
½ cup chopped peanuts	120 ml

- Preheat oven to 350° (176° C).

- Cream shortening, peanut butter, sugar and powdered sugar in large bowl. Beat in eggs and vanilla, gradually stir in flour and baking soda and mix well. Fold in chopped peanuts.

- Drop by teaspoonfuls onto cookie sheet and flatten slightly with fork.

- Bake for 10 minutes and watch closely so cookies will not brown too much around edges.

- Place on rack to cool. Store in airtight container.

BAKE SALE TIP:

Place cookies on plastic plate lined with white doilies and cover with plastic wrap.

Peanutty Pinwheels

1 (18 ounce) roll refrigerated sugar cookie dough	510 g
¼ cup flaked coconut	60 ml
1 (18 ounce) roll refrigerated peanut butter cookie dough	510 g
1 cup very finely chopped peanuts	240 ml

- Preheat oven to 375° (190° C).

- Combine sugar cookie dough and coconut in large mixing bowl and mix well with wooden spoon. Divide dough in half.

- Divide peanut butter cookie dough in half. Roll each half dough into 12 x 6-inch (32 x 15 cm) rectangle between pieces of wax paper. Remove top piece of wax paper and invert 1 rectangle on top of the other. Press down gently to seal.

- With peanut butter dough on bottom, tightly roll jelly-roll style from long side and repeat with remaining dough portions.

- Sprinkle half chopped peanuts onto wax paper and roll 1 log of dough in peanuts. Wrap in plastic wrap and repeat with remaining dough and peanuts. Chill dough logs at least 1 hour or until firm enough to slice.

- Use sharp, thin knife to cut slices ¼-inch (.6 cm) thick and place on cookie sheet 2 inches (5 cm) apart.

- Bake for 10 minutes or until edges are firm. Cool completely before packaging.

Fast Money!
Single-Serving
Bars & Squares

Apricot-Oatmeal Bars

1 (18 ounce) box yellow cake mix	510 g
3 cups oats	710 ml
¾ cup chopped pecans	180 ml
1 egg, slightly beaten	
1 cup (2 sticks) butter, melted	240 ml
1 (16 ounce) jar apricot preserves	.5 kg

- Preheat oven to 350° (176° C).

- Combine cake mix, oats, pecans, egg and melted butter and mix until batter is crumbly. Press half mixture evenly in 9 x 13-inch (23 x 33 cm) sprayed baking pan.

- Place apricot preserves in saucepan and heat just enough to be able to spread evenly over crust. Sprinkle remaining half of crust mixture over preserves. Bake for 25 minutes or until top is light brown.

Honey-Nut Bars

⅓ cup (⅔ stick) butter	80 ml
¼ cup cocoa	60 ml
1 (10 ounce) package miniature marshmallows	280 g
6 cups honey-nut clusters cereal	1.5 L

- Melt butter in large saucepan and stir in cocoa and marshmallows. Cook over low heat, stirring constantly, until marshmallows melt and mixture is smooth.

- Remove from heat and stir in honey-nut cereal.

- Pour into 7 x 11-inch (18 x 28 cm) sprayed pan. With spatula, smooth mixture in pan. Cool completely and cut into bars.

Rainbow Bars

2 large eggs, beaten
1¼ cups sugar   300 ml
¾ cup (1½ sticks) butter   180 ml
1 teaspoon vanilla   5 ml
2½ cups miniature colored marshmallows   540 ml
32 graham crackers, crushed
½ cup flaked coconut   120 ml
½ cup colored M&M's®   120 ml

- Combine eggs, sugar and butter in heavy saucepan over medium heat and cook, stirring constantly, until mixture thickens. Remove from heat and cool.

- Stir in vanilla, marshmallows, crackers, coconut and candies. Press into buttered 9 x 13-inch (23 x 33 cm) foil baking pan. When cool, cut into bars and chill until time to transfer to bake sale.

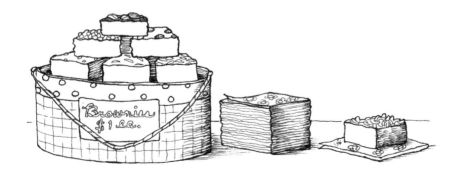

Rocky Road Bars

1 (12 ounce) package semi-sweet chocolate chips	340 g
1 (14 ounce) can sweetened condensed milk	396 g
2 tablespoons butter	30 ml
2 cups dry-roasted peanuts	480 ml
1 (10 ounce) package miniature marshmallows	280 g

- Place chocolate chips, sweetened condensed milk and butter in top of double boiler, heat until chocolate and butter melt and stir constantly.

- Remove from heat and stir in peanuts and marshmallows.

- Spread mixture quickly on wax paper-lined 9 x 13-inch (23 x 33 cm) pan.

- Chill at least 2 hours before cutting into bars. Store in refrigerator until time to transfer to bake sale.

BAKE SALE TIP:

Buyers won't be able to smell the fresh-baked goodies because of the wrapping. Make items visually appealing.

Toffee Bars

1½ cups (3 sticks) butter, softened	360 ml
2 cups packed light brown sugar	480 ml
2 teaspoons vanilla	10 ml
3 cups flour	710 ml
1 (8 ounce) package chocolate chips	227 g
¾ cup chopped chocolate-covered	
English toffee candy	180 ml

• Preheat oven to 350° (176° C).

• In mixing bowl, combine butter, brown sugar and vanilla and beat on medium speed for 3 minutes. Add flour, mix until they blend completely and stir in chocolate chips.

• Place dough on 9 x 13-inch (23 x 33 cm) sprayed, foil baking pan and bake for 30 minutes or until light brown. While bars are still hot, scatter chopped candy over bars. Cool and cut into bars. Cover with plastic wrap after they cool.

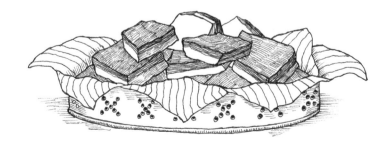

Rainbow Cookie Bars

*When making these one time, I
realized I was missing the M&M's®, so I substituted
white chocolate bits. They were great, just not "rainbow".*

½ cup (1 stick) butter	120 ml
2 cups graham cracker crumbs	480 ml
1 (14 ounce) can sweetened condensed milk	396 g
⅔ cup flaked coconut	160 ml
1 cup chopped pecans	240 ml
1 cup M&M's® plain chocolate candies	240 ml

- Preheat oven to 350° (176° C).

- In 9 x 13-inch (23 x 33 cm) foil baking pan, melt butter in oven.

- Sprinkle crumbs over butter and pour sweetened condensed milk over crumbs.

- Top with coconut, pecans and M&M's® and press down firmly.

- Bake for 25 to 30 minutes or until light brown. Cool and cut into bars.

Pineapple-Coconut Bars

1 (18 ounce) roll refrigerated sugar cookie dough	510 g
1 cup chopped pecans	240 ml
½ cup butterscotch chips	120 ml
½ cup coarsely chopped candied pineapple	120 ml
½ cup Craisins® (dried cranberries)	120 ml
½ cup flaked coconut	120 ml

- Preheat oven to 325° (162° C).

- Stir cookie dough in mixing bowl with wooden spoon until softened. Stir in pecans, chips, pineapple and cranberries and pat dough evenly in 9 x 13-inch (23 x 33 cm) sprayed, foil baking pan. Sprinkle coconut over top and press lightly.

- Bake for 20 minutes or until toothpick inserted near center comes out clean. Cool completely and cut into 24 bars.

BAKE SALE TIP:

For a nice touch place an additional piece of the candied pineapple on top of each bar.

Pineapple-Crumb Bars

1 (18 ounce) box yellow cake mix	510 g
½ cup (1 stick) butter, softened, divided	120 ml
1½ cups oats, divided	360 ml
1 large egg	
1 (20 ounce) can pineapple pie filling	567 g
⅓ cup packed brown sugar	80 ml

- Preheat oven to 350° (176° C).

- With mixer, beat cake mix, 5 tablespoons (75 ml) butter and 1 cup (240 ml) oats. Mix until crumbly and set aside 1 cup (240 ml) for topping.

- Combine egg and remaining mixture and stir well. Press into 9 x 13-inch (23 x 33 cm) sprayed, floured baking pan. Spread pineapple pie filling evenly over crust.

- In same bowl, combine remaining crumb mixture, remaining oats, 3 tablespoons (45 ml) butter and brown sugar and blend well. Sprinkle over pineapple filling and bake for 35 minutes or until light brown on top.

Polka-Dot Bars

2 cups flour	480 ml
1¼ cups packed brown sugar	300 ml
1 teaspoon baking powder	5 ml
¼ teaspoon baking soda	1 ml
¾ cup shortening	180 ml
2 eggs, beaten	
⅓ cup milk	80 ml
¾ cup miniature candy-coated	
chocolate pieces	180 ml

- Preheat oven to 350° (176° C).

- Combine flour, brown sugar, baking powder and baking soda, cut in shortening and mix well. Stir in eggs and milk and spread in 7 x 11-inch (18 x 28 cm) sprayed baking pan.

- Bake for 10 minutes, remove from oven and sprinkle candy pieces over top of partially baked bars. Return to oven for 10 to 15 minutes or until golden brown and firm around edges.

- Cool in pan and cut into 24 bars.

Lemon Bars

*You just can't have a bake sale without
several pans of lemon bars. Everyone loves lemon bars.*

1 cup (2 sticks) butter	240 ml
2 cups flour	480 ml
½ cup powdered sugar	120 ml
2 cups sugar	480 ml
6 tablespoons flour	90 ml
2 lemons	
4 eggs, lightly beaten	
Powdered sugar	

- Preheat oven to 350° (176° C).

- Melt butter in 9 x 13-inch (23 x 33 cm) baking pan in oven. Add flour and powdered sugar to mixture, stir and mix well. Press down evenly and firmly and bake for 15 minutes.

- For filling, combine sugar and flour in mixing bowl. Squeeze 6 tablespoons (90 ml) juice from lemons and grate ½ teaspoon (2 ml) rind. Add juice, rind and eggs and mix. Pour over crust.

- Bake for 20 minutes more. Cool and dust with powdered sugar. To serve, cut into squares.

BAKE SALE TIP:

Bake these in a 9 x 13-inch (23 x 33 cm) foil baking pan. Cool, cut into bars and cover pan with light yellow plastic wrap. Seal the bottom edges together with tape. It would be nice to have narrow yellow ribbon tied around the pan, like a gift.

Guess-What Bars

1 (10 ounce) bag original corn chips	280 g
1 cup sugar	240 ml
1⅓ cups light corn syrup	320 ml
1 cup creamy peanut butter	240 ml
½ cup chopped peanuts	120 ml
1⅓ cups white chocolate chips	320 ml

- Butter 9 x 13-inch (23 x 33 cm) baking dish. Crunch corn chips in bag and spread evenly over bottom of baking dish.

- In saucepan on medium heat, bring sugar and corn syrup to a boil or just until sugar dissolves completely. Remove from heat and stir in peanut butter until smooth.

- Immediately sprinkle peanuts and chocolate chips over corn syrup-peanut butter mixture and set aside until chips melt. Cut into large bars.

BAKE SALE TIP:

Wrap bars individually with plastic wrap. Seal wrap on underneath side with adhesive dot. (Buyers will eat these bars while shopping for other "goodies".)

Creamy-Crunchy Chocolate Bars

¾ cup whipping cream	180 ml
1 (12 ounce) package milk chocolate chips	340 g
4 cups miniature marshmallows	1 L
1 (7.5 ounce) package chocolate-covered	
graham crackers	210 g
¾ cup chopped pecans	180 ml
2 (1.5 ounce) bar milk chocolate bars	2 (45 g)

- Place whipping cream in large saucepan and heat over medium-low heat. Add chocolate chips and stir until chips melt. Remove from heat, add marshmallows and stir to coat.

- Break up graham crackers into bite-size pieces (not crushed), add pecans and gently stir into cream-marshmallow mixture. Spread into 9-inch (23 cm) foil-lined square pan. Cut into bars and place a bite-size piece of chocolate, vertically, on top of each bar.

- Refrigerate at least 3 hours or until firm. Cut into bars.

E TIP:

rs with plastic wrap and transport on a
king sheet to keep top from cracking.

Date-Pecan Bars

Filling:

2 (8 ounce) boxes pitted dates, chopped	2 (227 g)
1½ cups orange juice	360 ml
⅓ cup sugar	80 ml
¼ teaspoon ground cinnamon	1 ml

Crust and Topping:

1½ cups flour	360 ml
1½ cups quick-cooking oats	360 ml
¾ cup packed brown sugar	180 ml
1½ cups finely chopped pecans	360 ml
1¼ cups (2½ sticks) cold butter, cut up	300 ml

- In saucepan, combine dates, orange juice, sugar and cinnamon and bring to a boil. Reduce heat and simmer, stirring several times, for 15 minutes or until mixture thickens.

- Preheat oven to 350° (176° C).

- Spray, flour 9 x 13-inch (23 x 33 cm) foil pan. Place flour, oats, brown sugar and pecans in mixing bowl and cut in butter until mixture is crumbly.

- Transfer 2½ cups (600 ml) mixture to another bowl and set aside. Press remaining crumbs over bottom of prepared pan. Spoon filling over crust and spread up to ¼-inch (.6 cm) from edge. Sprinkle remaining crust mixture over top of filling and bake for 35 minutes.

Delicious Apricot Bars

1¼ cups flour	300 ml
1 cup oats	240 ml
½ cup packed brown sugar	120 ml
¼ teaspoon baking powder	1 ml
½ cup (1 stick) butter, softened	120 ml
1 cup apricot preserves	240 ml

- Preheat oven to 350° (176° C).

- Combine flour, oats, brown sugar and baking powder in large bowl. Cut in butter until it is crumbly. Remove 2 cups (480 ml) mixture and press evenly into 9 x 13-inch (23 x 33 cm) sprayed baking pan. Set aside remaining flour-sugar mixture.

- Place apricot preserves in saucepan, heat and stir just until mixture is spreadable. Spread, using back of tablespoon, apricot preserves to within ½-inch (1.2 cm) of pan's edge.

- Sprinkle on remaining crumbly crust mixture and gently press down. Bake for 25 minutes or until light brown. Cool and cut into bars.

BAKE SALE TIP:

Keep prices simple for adding and making change by pricing in increments of 25 cents. Be prepared with cash box with plenty of change, price stickers and marking pens.

Double Delicious Bars

½ cup (1 stick) butter	120 ml
1½ cups graham cracker crumbs	360 ml
1 (14 ounce) can sweetened condensed milk	396 g
1 (12 ounce) package semi-sweet chocolate chips	340 g
1 cup peanut butter chips	240 ml

- Preheat oven to 325° (162° C).

- In 9 x 13-inch (23 x 33 cm) baking dish, melt butter in oven. Sprinkle crumbs evenly over butter and pour sweetened condensed milk evenly over crumbs.

- Top with chocolate and peanut butter chips and press down firmly. Bake for 25 to 30 minutes or until light brown. Cool and cut into bars.

BAKE SALE TIP:

This is another easy recipe that could be cut in as many as 48 little bars and served to buyers to "whet their appetite" for other goodies.

Cranberry-Oat Bars

1 (12 ounce) package whole cranberries,	
rinsed	340 g
¾ cup sugar	180 ml
½ teaspoon cinnamon	2 ml
1½ cups flour	360 ml
1 teaspoon ground ginger	5 ml
1 teaspoon baking powder	5 ml
1 cup (2 sticks) butter, softened	240 ml
1 cup packed brown sugar	240 ml
2 large eggs	
1¾ cups oats	420 ml

• Combine cranberries, sugar, cinnamon and ¾ cup (180 ml) water in saucepan. Cook over medium heat until all cranberries "burst" and mixture thickens, about 10 minutes. Transfer to bowl and refrigerate until cool and thick.

• Preheat oven to 350° (176° C).

• Combine flour, ginger, baking powder and set aside. In mixing bowl, beat butter and brown sugar until light and fluffy. Add eggs, 1 at a time and beat after each addition. Stir in dry ingredients and oats.

• Reserve 1½ cups (360 ml) mixture for topping. Spread remaining dough 9 x 13-inch (23 x 33 cm) sprayed foil baking pan. Spoon cranberry filling evenly over dough.

• Put flour on and sprinkle small clumps of reserved dough over cranberries. Bake for 35 to 40 minutes or until top is golden brown. Cool several hours before cutting into bars.

Coconut-Brownie Bars

2 (18 ounce) tubes chocolate chip cookie dough	2 (510 g)
2 eggs, slightly beaten	
⅓ cup oil	80 ml
1 (18 ounce) box brownie mix	510 g
1 cup chopped walnuts	240 ml
1 cup flaked coconut	240 ml
1 (16 ounce) carton coconut-pecan icing	.5 kg

- Preheat oven to 350° (176° C).

- Press cookie dough into 10 x 14-inch (25 x 36 cm) sprayed jelly-roll pan. In large bowl, combine eggs, oil, brownie mix and ¼ cup (60 ml) water and mix until they blend well. Spoon brownie mixture over cookie dough. Sprinkle with walnuts and coconut.

- Bake for 55 minutes. Cool and place thin layer of icing over bars.

BAKE SALE TIP:

Place bars on plastic platter lined with paper doily and cover with plastic wrap.

Chocolate-Pecan Bars

2 cups flour	480 ml
1 teaspoon vanilla	5 ml
1 cup packed brown sugar	240 ml
½ cup shortening	120 ml
½ cup (1 stick) butter, softened	120 ml
1 egg yolk, beaten	
6 (1.45 ounce) Hershey® bars	6 (45 g)
¾ cup chopped pecans	180 ml

- Preheat oven to 350° (176° C).

- Combine all ingredients except Hershey® bars and pecans and spread on 9 x 13-inch (23 x 33 cm) sprayed foil baking pan. Bake for 15 to 20 minutes.

- While bars are still hot, break up Hershey® bars in small pieces, scatter over baked bars and cover with pecans. Cut while warm. Cool completely and cover with plastic wrap.

  TIP: Transport bars on level baking sheet to keep foil pan from bending.

BAKE SALE TIP:

Look at discount stores for inexpensive containers for your "goodies" at the bake sale. I found a packet of 5 plastic squares and round containers with lids that holds 5 cups (1.3 L) for $1.

Chocolate-Ribbon Bars

½ cup (1 stick) butter, melted	120 ml
1 (18 ounce) box yellow cake mix	510 g
1 (5 ounce) can evaporated milk	143 g
1 cup chopped pecans	240 ml
1 cup caramel ice cream topping	240 ml
1½ cups chocolate chips	360 ml

- Preheat oven to 350° (176° C).

- In mixing bowl, combine and mix butter, cake mix and evaporated milk and stir in pecans. Spoon half batter into 9 x 13-inch (23 x 33 cm) sprayed, floured foil baking pan and bake for about 12 minutes. Remove pan from oven, drizzle caramel topping over cake mixture and sprinkle chocolate chips evenly over batter. Drop remaining batter on top by spoonfuls and return to oven for another 25 minutes or until slightly golden.

BAKE SALE TIP:

Bars can be displayed in pan with plastic wrap. Be sure to carry bars on flat surface like a baking sheet so bars will not crack on top. Another way to display bars is to cut into large pieces and wrap individually.

Chocolate-Butter Bars

1 (18 ounce) box German chocolate cake mix	510 g
½ cup packed brown sugar	120 ml
1 egg	
¼ cup milk	60 ml
½ cup plus 2 tablespoons creamy peanut butter, divided	120 ml/30 ml
2 tablespoons butter	30 ml
3 tablespoons light corn syrup	45 ml
1 cup milk chocolate chips	240 ml
⅓ cup powdered sugar	80 ml

- Preheat oven to 325° (162° C).

- Use mixer to beat cake mix, brown sugar, egg and milk and mix well. Stir in ½ cup (120 ml) creamy peanut butter. Pour into 9 x 13-inch (23 x 33 cm) sprayed, floured baking pan and bake for 25 to 30 minutes or until toothpick inserted in center comes out clean.

- For frosting, heat butter, 2 tablespoons (30 ml) peanut butter and corn syrup in saucepan and stir frequently until mixture is smooth. Remove from heat, stir in chocolate chips and beat until mixture is smooth. Add powdered sugar and mix well. Ice bars with frosting.

Chocolate Chip-Cheese Bars

1 (18 ounce) tube refrigerated chocolate chip cookie dough	510 g
1 (8 ounce) package cream cheese, softened	227 g
½ cup sugar	120 ml
1 egg	

- Preheat oven to 350° (176° C).

- Cut cookie dough in half.

- Press half dough into bottom of sprayed 9-inch (23 cm) square baking pan or 7 x 11-inch (18 x 28 cm) baking pan.

- In mixing bowl, beat cream cheese, sugar and egg until smooth. Spread mixture over crust and crumble remaining dough over top.

- Bake for 35 to 40 minutes or until toothpick inserted near center comes out clean.

- Cool on wire rack and cut into bars.

Chocolate Chip-Coconut Bars

These are sinfully rich bars.

1 (18 ounce) box German chocolate cake mix	510 g
3 cups oats	710 ml
1 cup (2 sticks) butter, melted	240 ml
1 (14 ounce) can sweetened condensed milk	396 g
1 cup milk chocolate chips	240 ml
1 cup flaked coconut	240 ml
1 cup chopped walnuts	240 ml

- Preheat oven to 375° (190° C)

- Combine cake mix and oats. Add butter and beat on low speed 1 minute and until they blend well. Spoon half cake mixture into 9 x 13-inch (23 x 33 cm) sprayed, floured foil baking pan and spread evenly in pan. Pour sweetened condensed milk evenly over batter.

- Sprinkle chocolate chips and coconut evenly over sweetened condensed milk. Combine remaining half cake mixture with chopped walnuts, mix well and crumble over chips and coconut. Bake for 20 minutes. Cool before slicing into bars.

TIP: These bars are quite rich without a frosting, but for a bake sale, it could use a frosting. Buy 1 (16 ounce .5 kg) can triple chocolate fudge frosting.

Gooey Good Turtle Bars

½ cup (1 stick) butter, melted	120 ml
2 cups vanilla wafer crumbs	480 ml
1 (12 ounce) semi-sweet chocolate chips	340 g
1 cup pecan pieces	240 ml
1 (12 ounce) jar caramel topping	340 g

- Preheat oven to 350° (176° C).

- Combine butter and wafer crumbs in 9 x 13-inch (23 x 33 cm) baking pan and press into bottom of pan. Sprinkle with chocolate chips and pecans.

- Remove lid from caramel topping, microwave on HIGH for 30 seconds or until hot and drizzle over pecans.

- Bake for about 15 minutes or until chocolate chips melt.

- Cool in pan and chill at least 30 minutes before cutting into squares.

    TIP: Watch bars closely – so chips melt, but crumbs do not burn.

BAKE SALE TIP:

These bars are so easy to make, you might want to bake an extra batch to cut into smaller bars and hand out as samples. When people get a bite, they will know they are at a great bake sale.

Chocolate-Coconut Bars

1 (17.6 ounce) box brownie mix	484 g
1 large egg	
⅓ cup oil	80 ml
½ cup flaked coconut	120 ml
½ cup miniature chocolate chips	120 ml
¾ sugar	180 ml
⅓ cup (⅔ stick) butter	80 ml
1 (5 ounce) can evaporated milk	143 g
1 egg, beaten	
1 cup flaked coconut	240 ml
1 cup chopped pecans	240 ml

- Preheat oven to 350° (176° C).

- Stir brownie mix, egg, oil and ¼ cup (60 ml) water in large bowl and mix well. Stir in coconut and chocolate chips and spread in 9 x 13-inch (23 x 33 cm) sprayed baking pan. Bake for 20 to 25 minutes or until center is firm.

- Combine sugar, butter, evaporated milk and egg in saucepan over medium-high heat, cook about 15 minutes and whisk until bubbly and thick. Stir in coconut and pecans and cook another 2 minutes.

- While bars are still hot, pour sugar-pecan mixture over top and spread to edges. Cool completely before slicing into bars.

Chocolate-Oatmeal Bars

½ cup quick-cooking oatmeal	120 ml
¼ cup (½ stick) butter, softened	60 ml
½ cup sugar	120 ml
½ cup packed brown sugar	120 ml
1 egg	
¾ cup flour	180 ml
1 tablespoon cocoa	15 ml
½ teaspoon baking soda	2 ml
1 (6 ounce) package chocolate chips	168 g
½ cup chopped pecans	120 ml

- Preheat oven to 350° (176° C).

- Combine oatmeal with ¾ cup (180 ml) boiling water and let stand 10 minutes. In separate bowl, cream butter, sugars and egg and mix well.

- Stir in dry ingredients with ¼ teaspoon (1 ml) salt and blend in oatmeal. Add half chocolate chips and spread batter in 9 x 9-inch (23 x 23 cm) sprayed, floured baking pan. Sprinkle remaining chips and pecans on top of batter. Bake for 30 to 35 minutes.

BAKE SALE TIP:

Make brownies (made from a mix) in different shaped pans. Creativity can sell simple items.

Chocolate-Cherry Bars

1 (18 ounce) devil's food cake mix	510 g
1 (20 ounce) can cherry pie filling	567 g
2 eggs	
1 cup milk chocolate chips	240 ml

Frosting for Bars:

1 (3 ounce) square semi-sweet chocolate, melted	84 g
1 (3 ounce) package cream cheese, softened	84 g
½ teaspoon vanilla	2 ml
1½ cups powdered sugar	360 ml

- Preheat oven to 350° (176° C).

- In large bowl, mix cake mix, pie filling, eggs and chocolate chips by hand and blend well.

- Pour batter into 9 x 13-inch (23 x 33 cm) sprayed, floured baking dish.

- Bake for 25 to 30 minutes or until toothpick inserted in center comes out clean. Cool.

- In medium bowl beat chocolate, cream cheese and vanilla until smooth. Gradually beat in powdered sugar. Pour over bars.

Caramel-Chocolate Chip Bars

1 (18 ounce) package caramel cake mix	510 g
2 eggs	
⅓ cup firmly packed light brown sugar	80 ml
¼ cup (½ stick) butter, softened	60 ml
1 cup semi-sweet chocolate chips	240 ml
1 (16 ounce) carton caramel frosting	.5 kg

- Preheat oven to 350° (176° C).

- Combine cake mix, eggs, ¼ cup (60 ml) water, brown sugar and butter in large bowl. Stir until it blends thoroughly. (Mixture will be thick.)

- Stir in chocolate chips. Spread in 9 x 13-inch (23 x 33 cm) sprayed, floured baking pan.

- Bake for about 25 to 30 minutes or until toothpick inserted in center comes out clean. Cool and cut into squares.

BAKE SALE TIP:

These bars are especially good when frosted. Use a caramel frosting to save time. It might help sales to buy 1 (12 ounce/340 g) package Milky Way PoPables®, place 1 in center of every square and press down just a little. The caramel center of these balls are great on these caramel-chocolate bars.

Goody Bag

Banana-Cream Bars

½ cup (1 stick) butter, softened   120 ml
1½ cups sugar   360 ml
2 large eggs
2 teaspoons vanilla   10 ml
¾ cup sour cream   180 ml
2 large or 3 medium bananas, mashed
2 cups flour   480 ml
1 teaspoon baking soda   5 ml
Sweet butter cream icing

• Preheat oven to 350° (176° C).

• Cream butter and sugar, add unbeaten eggs and beat
  thoroughly. Stir in vanilla and sour cream and mix
  well. Add dry ingredients with ¼ teaspoon (1 ml) salt
  alternately with mashed bananas and mix until they
  blend well.

• Spoon into 10 x 15-inch (25 x 38 cm) sprayed baking
  pan and bake for 25 to 30 minutes. Cool. Spread with
  Sweet Butter Cream Icing on page 100.

BAKE SALE TIP:

*Take these bars to the bake sale in foil pan on metal
baking sheet so top doesn't crack. Cut into bars and
cover with plastic wrap.*

Butter-Pecan Turtle Bars

2 cups flour	480 ml
1½ cups packed light brown sugar, divided	360 ml
1½ cups (3 sticks) butter, divided	360 ml
1½ cups lightly chopped pecans	360 ml
4 squares semi-sweet chocolate	

• Preheat oven to 350° (176° C).

• In large mixing bowl, combine flour, ¾ cup (180 ml) brown sugar and ½ cup (120 ml) butter and blend until crumbly.

• Pat down crust mixture evenly in 9 x 13-inch (23 x 33 cm) sprayed baking pan. Sprinkle pecans over crust and set aside.

• To make a caramel sauce, combine ¾ cup (180 ml) packed brown sugar and ¾ cup (180 ml) butter in small saucepan. Cook over medium heat and stir constantly. Bring mixture to a boil for 1 minute and stir constantly.

• Drizzle caramel sauce over pecans and crust and bake for 18 to 20 minutes or until caramel layer bubbles. Remove from oven and cool.

• In saucepan, melt chocolate squares and ¼ cup (60 ml) butter and stir until smooth. Pour over bars and spread around. Cool and cut into bars.

Apricot-Almond Bars

1 (18 ounce) package yellow cake mix	510 g
½ cup (1 stick) butter, melted	120 ml
¾ cup finely chopped almonds	180 ml
1 (12 ounce) jar apricot preserves, divided, warmed	340 g
1 (8 ounce) package cream cheese, softened	227 g
¼ cup sugar	60 ml
2 tablespoons flour	30 ml
1 egg	
1 teaspoon vanilla	5 ml
⅔ cup flaked coconut	160 ml

- Preheat oven to 350° (176° C).

- In large bowl, combine cake mix and butter and mix by hand just until crumbly.

- Stir in almonds and set aside 1 cup (240 ml) crumb mixture. Lightly press remaining crumb mixture into 9 x 13-inch (23 x 33 cm) sprayed, floured baking pan.

- Carefully spread 1 cup (240 ml) preserves over crumb mixture, but leave ¼-inch (.6 cm) border.

- Beat cream cheese with mixer until smooth. Add remaining preserves, sugar, flour, ⅛ teaspoon (.5 ml) salt, egg and vanilla and beat well.

- Carefully spread cream cheese mixture over top of preserves.

- Combine saved 1 cup (240 ml) crumb mixture and coconut and mix well. Sprinkle over cream cheese mixture.

- Bake for 35 minutes or until center sets. Cool and store in refrigerator.

Almond-Coconut Squares

2 cups graham cracker crumbs	480 ml
3 tablespoons brown sugar	45 ml
½ cup (1 stick) butter, melted	120 ml
1 (14 ounce) can sweetened condensed milk	396 g
1 (7 ounce) package flaked coconut	198 g
1 teaspoon vanilla	5 ml

Topping:

1 (6 ounce) package chocolate chips	168 g
1 (6 ounce) package butterscotch chips	168 g
¼ cup (½ stick) butter	60 ml
6 tablespoons chunky peanut butter	90 ml
½ cup slivered almonds	120 ml

- Preheat oven to 325° (162° C).

- Mix graham cracker crumbs, brown sugar and butter. Pat into 9 x 13-inch (23 x 33 cm) sprayed baking pan. Bake for 10 minutes and cool.

- Combine sweetened condensed milk, coconut and vanilla. Pour over baked crust, bake another 25 minutes and cool.

- For topping, melt ingredients in top of double boiler. Spread over baked ingredients. Cool and cut into squares.

BAKE SALE TIP:

These squares can be cut into large squares and wrapped individually, but the easiest way to present them is to bake in 9 x 13-inch (23 x 33 cm) foil pan, cut into squares and cover with plastic wrap. These squares are irresistible when you stick a whole almond on top of each square.

Butterscotch Squares

1 (18 ounce) box yellow cake mix	510 g
1 (3.4 ounce) package instant butterscotch pudding mix	100 g
1 cup milk	240 ml
1 egg, slightly beaten	
1 teaspoon vanilla	5 ml
½ cup butterscotch chips	120 ml
½ cup peanut butter chips	120 ml
1 cup chopped pecans	240 ml

- Preheat oven to 350° (176° C).

- Combine cake mix, pudding mix, milk, egg and vanilla in large bowl. Beat on low-medium speed about 1 minute or until they blend well.

- Stir in butterscotch chips and peanut butter chips and pour into 9 x 13-inch (23 x 33 cm) sprayed, floured baking pan. Sprinkle pecans over top of squares and bake for 30 to 35 minutes or until toothpick inserted in center comes out clean.

BAKE SALE TIP:

These butterscotch squares are great without icing, but if you want icing, use 1 (16 ounce/.5 kg) carton butter cream icing and sprinkle a few more butterscotch chips over top of icing.

Buttery Walnut Squares

1 cup (2 sticks) butter, softened	240 ml
1¾ cups packed brown sugar	420 ml
1¾ cups flour	420 ml

Topping:

1 cup packed brown sugar	240 ml
4 eggs, lightly beaten	
2 tablespoons flour	30 ml
2 cups chopped walnuts	480 ml
1 cup flaked coconut	240 ml

- Preheat oven to 350° (176° C).

- In bowl, combine butter and sugar and beat until smooth and creamy. Add flour and mix well. Pat mixture down evenly in 9 x 13-inch (23 x 33 cm) sprayed baking pan and bake for 15 minutes.

- For topping, combine sugar and eggs in medium bowl. Add flour and mix well. Fold in walnuts and coconut and pour over crust. Bake for 20 to 25 minutes or until is firm in center. Cool in pan and cut into squares.

BAKE SALE TIP:

When you bake recipes for bake sales, use foil baking pans so buyers can keep them. Just be sure to carry the foil pan on metal baking sheet so top doesn't crack.

Another way to sell squares is to cut them a little larger and individually wrap each square. Cut several squares into small pieces for "taste tests".

Chocolate-Caramel Squares

1 (18 ounce) box chocolate cake mix	510 g
¾ cup (1½ sticks) butter, softened	180 ml
1 egg, slightly beaten	
2 cups quick-cooking oats	480 ml
1 (14 ounce) bag caramels, unwrapped	396 g
¼ cup milk	60 ml
½ cup milk chocolate chips	120 ml
¾ cup slivered almonds	180 ml

- Preheat oven to 350° (176° C).

- Combine cake mix, butter and egg in mixing bowl and beat on low speed until they blend well. Stir in oats and use your hands to mix dough well.

- Reserve 1½ cups (360 ml) cake mixture and set aside. Press remaining mixture into 9 x 13-inch (23 x 33 cm) sprayed baking pan. (You may have to spray back of large spoon to press mixture evenly in pan. Dough will be sticky.)

- In heavy saucepan, heat caramels and milk over low-medium heat and stir constantly until caramels melt. Pour melted caramels over chocolate layer in pan and sprinkle with chocolate chips and almonds.

- Sprinkle reserved cake mixture over top and bake for 24 to 28 minutes or until caramel bubbles along edges and cake mixture on top appears crisp and dry. Run knife around sides of pan to loosen bars and cool completely.

Chocolate-Cherry Squares

1 (4 ounce) package cook-and-serve chocolate pudding mix	114 g
1¾ cups milk	420 ml
¼ cup maraschino cherry juice	60 ml
1 (18 ounce) package chocolate cake mix	510 g
1 (10 ounce) jar chopped maraschino cherries	280 g
1 cup chocolate chips	240 ml
1 cup chopped pecans	240 ml

- Preheat oven to 350° (176° C).

- In saucepan, cook pudding mix, milk and cherry juice according to pudding directions.

- Stir pudding mixture into cake mix and cherries. Spread into 10 x 15-inch (25 x 38 cm) sprayed, floured baking pan. Sprinkle with chocolate chips and pecans and bake for 30 minutes.

BAKE SALE TIP:

These squares do not need icing. Cut in large 4 x 4-inch (10 x 10 cm) squares, wrap each square in different light colors of plastic wrap and place on plastic tray. Decorate with some Milky Way PoPables® in between squares. They'll look great.

Mint-Chocolate Squares

2 cups crushed chocolate-sandwich cookies	480 ml
1¼ cups chopped walnuts	300 ml
1 cup flaked coconut	240 ml
1½ cups mint-flavored chocolate chips	360 ml
1 teaspoon vanilla	5 ml
1 (14 ounce) can sweetened condensed milk	396 g

- Preheat oven to 350° (176° C).

- Spread chocolate cookie crumbs evenly onto 9 x 13-inch (23 x 33 cm) sprayed foil baking pan. Spread evenly with walnuts, coconut and mint-chocolate chips.

- Drizzle evenly with vanilla and sweetened condensed milk. Bake for 20 to 25 minutes. Cool in pan and cut into squares. Refrigerate until time for bake sale.

Coconut-Cherry Squares

This is not only pretty, it's good, good, good!

1⅓ cups plus ¾ cup flour, divided	320 ml/ 180 ml
⅔ cup (1¼ sticks) butter, softened	160 ml
1½ cups powdered sugar	360 ml

Filling:

3 eggs, beaten	
1½ cups sugar	360 ml
¾ teaspoon baking powder	4 ml
1 teaspoon vanilla	5 ml
¾ cup chopped pecans	180 ml
¾ cup flaked coconut	180 ml
¾ cup maraschino cherries, drained, chopped	180 ml

- Preheat oven to 350° (176° C). In mixing bowl, combine 1⅓ cups (320 ml) flour, butter and powdered sugar press into 9 x 13-inch (23 x 33 cm) baking pan.

- Bake for 20 minutes or just until golden and set aside.

- For filling, use same mixing bowl, combine eggs, sugar, baking powder, vanilla, ½ teaspoon (2 ml) salt and ¾ cup (180 ml) flour and mix well. Stir in pecans, coconut and cherries.

- Spread over crust and bake for 25 minutes or until golden brown. Cool and cut into squares.

BAKE SALE TIP:

For a holiday look use half green and half red maraschino cherries.

Pecan Squares

2 cups flour	480 ml
½ cup powdered sugar	120 ml
1 cup (2 sticks) butter, cut up	240 ml
1 (14 ounce) can sweetened condensed milk	396 g
2 eggs	
1 teaspoon vanilla	5 ml
1 (7.5 ounce) package Bits O'Brickle® chips	210 g
1 cup chopped pecans	240 ml

• Preheat oven to 350° (176° C).

• Combine flour and powdered sugar in medium bowl and mix well.

• Cut in butter with pastry blender or fork until crumbly. Press mixture evenly into 9 x 13-inch (23 x 33 cm) sprayed foil baking pan and bake for 15 minutes.

• Combine sweetened condensed milk, eggs, vanilla, Bits O'Brickle® and chopped pecans and pour over prepared crust. Bake for 25 minutes or until golden brown.

• Cool and cut into squares.

Pecan-Cream Cheese Squares

1 (18 ounce) package yellow cake mix	510 g
3 eggs, divided	
½ cup (1 stick) butter, softened	120 ml
2 cups chopped pecans	480 ml
1 (8 ounce) package cream cheese, softened	227 g
3⅔ cups powdered sugar	870 ml

- Preheat oven to 350° (176° C).

- In mixing bowl, combine cake mix, 1 egg and butter. Stir in pecans and mix well. Press into 9 x 13-inch (23 x 33 cm) sprayed baking pan.

- In mixing bowl, beat cream cheese, sugar and remaining eggs until smooth. Pour over pecan mixture.

- Bake for 55 minutes or until golden brown. Cool and cut into squares.

BAKE SALE TIP:

These squares are very rich and really need no icing. If you want to dress them up, use 1 (16 ounce/.5 kg) carton rainbow chip frosting. Ice the squares the day before the bake sale so the icing will not stick to plastic wrap. Chill until time for sale.

Squares to Love

4 cups round oat cereal	1 L
3 cups rice crispy cereal	710 ml
3 cups M&M's®	710 ml
1 (12 ounce) jar honey-roasted peanuts	340 g
1½ cups light corn syrup	360 ml
1¼ cups sugar	300 ml
1¾ cups creamy peanut butter	420 ml
1 teaspoon vanilla	5 ml

- Place oat cereal, rice cereal, M&M's® and peanuts in very large bowl. In saucepan, combine corn syrup and sugar, bring to a boil and stir frequently.

- Remove from heat and stir in peanut butter and vanilla. Pour over cereal mixture and toss to coat evenly. Spread into 10 x 15-inch (25 x 38 cm) sprayed baking pan.

- Use back of large spoon to spread cereal mixture evenly over pan. Let set an hour or two and cut into large squares.

BAKE SALE TIP:

These squares should be wrapped individually for individual sales. A single layer of plastic shows off the baked goods the best. A double layer of plastic wrap clouds the view.

Strawberry-Fudge Brownies

1 (19 ounce) box fudge brownie mix	538 g
½ cup oil	120 ml
2 eggs	
1 cup frozen strawberries, thawed, drained	240 ml
½ cup chopped pecans	120 ml
½ cup slivered almonds	120 ml
⅔ cup flaked coconut	160 ml
½ cup prepared fudge ice cream topping	120 ml

- Preheat oven to 325° (162° C).

- Beat in mixing bowl, brownie mix, oil, eggs and ½ cup (120 ml) water and mix well. Stir in strawberries and beat 2 minutes longer.

- Stir in pecans, almonds and coconut and spread batter in 9 x 13-inch (23 x 33 cm) sprayed, floured foil baking pan. Bake for 40 to 45 minutes or until toothpick inserted in center comes out almost clean.

- Drizzle fudge ice cream topping over cooled brownies. Let stand at least 2 hours before cutting into bars.

Glazed Butterscotch Brownies

3 cups packed brown sugar	710 ml
1 cup (2 sticks) butter, softened	240 ml
3 eggs	
3 cups flour	710 ml
2 tablespoons baking powder	30 ml
1½ cups chopped pecans	360 ml
1 cup flaked coconut	240 ml

Glaze:

½ cup packed brown sugar	120 ml
⅓ cup evaporated milk	80 ml
½ cup (1 stick) butter	120 ml
1 cup powdered sugar	240 ml
½ teaspoon vanilla	2 ml

- Preheat oven to 350° (176° C).

- Cream sugar and butter with mixer until fluffy. Add eggs and blend.

- Sift flour, baking powder and ½ teaspoon (2 ml) salt and add to other mixture 1 cup (240 ml) at a time. Add pecans and coconut.

- Spread batter into large 11 x 17-inch (30 x 42 cm) sprayed pan and bake for 20 to 25 minutes. (Batter will be hard to spread.)

- In saucepan, combine brown sugar, milk, butter and ⅛ teaspoon (.5 ml) salt and bring to a boil.

- Cool slightly and add powdered sugar and vanilla and beat until smooth. Spread over cooled brownies.

German Sweet Chocolate Brownies

1 (4 ounce) package German sweet chocolate   114 g
¼ cup (½ stick) butter   60 ml
¾ cup plus ¼ cup sugar   180 ml/60 ml
3 eggs, divided
1 teaspoon vanilla   5 ml
½ cup plus 1 tablespoon flour, divided   120 ml/15 ml
½ cup chopped pecans   120 ml
½ (8 ounce) package cream cheese, softened   ½ (227 g)

- Preheat oven to 350° (176° C).

- In glass bowl, microwave chocolate and butter until chocolate melts completely and blends well. Stir in ¾ cup (180 ml) sugar, 2 eggs and vanilla and mix until they blend completely.

- Mix in ½ cup (120 ml) flour until it blends well and add pecans. Spread in 8-inch (20 cm) sprayed foil baking pan.

- In same bowl, beat cream cheese, ¼ cup (60 ml) sugar, 1 egg and 1 tablespoon (15 ml) flour and mix until smooth. Spoon over brownie mixture and swirl with knife to form ribbons throughout mixture.

- Bake for 30 minutes or until toothpick inserted in center comes out clean. Cool in pan and cut into squares.

  TIP: This recipe can easily be doubled using a 9 x 13-inch (23 x 33 cm) pan and baked for about 40 minutes.

Chewy Caramel Brownies

1 (14 ounce) package unwrapped caramels	396 g
1 (5 ounce) can evaporated milk, divided	143 g
1 (18 ounce) box German chocolate cake mix	510 g
¾ cup (1½ sticks) butter, melted	180 ml
1 cup chopped pecans	240 ml
1 cup semi-sweet chocolate chips	240 ml

- Preheat oven to 350° (176° C).

- In saucepan over low heat, melt caramels with ⅓ cup (80 ml) evaporated milk. Stir constantly.

- In mixing bowl, combine cake mix with melted butter and stir in remaining milk. Spread half cake mixture into 9 x 13-inch (23 x 33 cm) sprayed foil baking pan and bake for 7 minutes. Sprinkle with pecans and chocolate chips and spoon on melted caramels.

- Drop spoonfuls of remaining cake mixture over top and lightly spread with back of spoon. Bake for 18 to 20 minutes and cool completely before cutting into squares.

BAKE SALE TIP:

Use bows, ribbons, colored plastic paper, special plates; but most of all, use your imagination.

Snickers® Brownies

1 (18 ounce) German chocolate cake mix	510 g
¾ cup (1½ sticks) butter, melted	180 ml
½ cup evaporated milk	120 ml
4 (3 ounce) Snickers® candy bars, cut in	
⅛-inch (.4 cm) slices	4 (84 g)

- Preheat oven to 350° (176° C).

- Combine cake mix, butter and evaporated milk in large bowl. Beat on low speed until mixture blends well.

- Pour half batter in 9 x 13-inch (23 x 33 cm) sprayed, floured foil baking pan. Bake for 10 minutes.

- Remove from oven and place candy bar slices evenly over brownies. Drop remaining half of batter by spoonfuls over candy bars and spread as evenly as possible.

- Place back in oven and bake for 20 minutes longer. When cool, cut into bars.

BAKE SALE TIP:

Label (typed) each food item on multi-colored paper or the colors of your theme!!

Cashew Brownies

1 (19.5 ounce) box traditional fudge brownie mix	538 g
¼ cup oil	60 ml
1 egg, slightly beaten	
1 cup milk chocolate chips	240 ml
1 (16 ounce) carton cream cheese icing	.5 kg
1 cup salted, coarsely chopped cashews	240 ml

- Preheat oven to 350° (176° C).

- Combine brownie mix, ⅓ cup (80 ml) water, oil and egg in large bowl and mix well. Stir in chocolate chips and pour into 9 x 13-inch (23 x 33 cm) sprayed, floured baking pan.

- Bake for about 26 minutes or until toothpick inserted in center comes out clean. Cool on wire rack.

- Spread cream cheese icing over brownies and sprinkle chopped cashews on top.

- Cut brownies in squares, place on plastic tray and cover with plastic wrap.

Classic Fudge Brownies

1 (18 ounce) box brownie classic fudge mix	510 g
½ cup oil	120 ml
2 eggs, slightly beaten	
1 cup chocolate chips	240 ml
1 cup chopped pecans	240 ml

- Preheat oven to 350° (176° C).

- Combine brownie mix, oil, eggs and ¼ cup (60 ml) water and mix well. Pour into 9 x 13-inch (23 x 33 cm) sprayed, floured baking dish. In small bowl, combine chocolate chips and pecans and sprinkle over batter.

- Bake for 25 to 30 minutes.

BAKE SALE TIP:

An icing is not really needed for these brownies, however when this is made for a bake sale, I would ice with 1 (16 ounce /.5 kg) can creamy milk chocolate icing.

Easy Blonde Brownies

This is another one of those recipes that seems too easy. You already have everything right in the pantry.

1 (1 pound) box light brown sugar	.5 kg
4 eggs	
2 cups biscuit mix	480 ml
2 cups chopped pecans	480 ml

- Preheat oven to 350° (176° C).

- Use mixer to beat brown sugar, eggs and biscuit mix. Stir in pecans and pour into 9 x 13-inch (23 x 33 cm) sprayed baking pan.

- Bake for 35 minutes. Cool and cut into squares.

Chocolate-Peanut Pizza

1 (18 ounce) roll refrigerated sugar cookie dough	510 g
⅔ cup creamy peanut butter	160 ml
1 cup peanut butter chips	240 ml
1 cup miniature candy-coated chocolate pieces	240 ml

- Preheat oven to 350° (176° C).

- Spread dough evenly on bottom and up sides of 12-inch (32 cm) sprayed pizza pan. Bake on bottom rack for 20 minutes or until crust is golden brown. Cool for 15 minutes.

- Spread peanut butter evenly on top of cookie crust and sprinkle with peanut butter chips and chocolate pieces. Cut into wedges to serve.

Almond-Fudge Shortbread

1 cup (2 sticks) butter, softened	240 ml
½ cup powdered sugar	120 ml
1¼ cups flour	300 ml
1 (12 ounce) package chocolate chips	340 g
1 (14 ounce) can sweetened condensed milk	396 g
½ teaspoon almond extract	2 ml
1 (2.5 ounce) package almonds, toasted	70 g

- Preheat oven to 350° (176° C).

- In mixing bowl, beat butter, sugar and ¼ teaspoon (1 ml) salt.

- Stir in flour, pat into 9 x 13-inch (23 x 33 cm) sprayed baking pan and bake for 15 minutes.

- In medium saucepan over low heat, melt chocolate chips with sweetened condensed milk and stir constantly until chips melt.

- Stir in almond extract, spread evenly over shortbread and sprinkle with almonds.

- Chill several hours or until firm. Cut into bars. Bars may be stored at room temperature.

BAKE SALE TIP:

Take these bars to the bake sale in foil pan on metal baking sheet so top doesn't crack. Cut into bars and cover with plastic wrap.

Goody Bag

Carmelitas

Crust:

1 cup flour	240 ml
¾ cup packed brown sugar	180 ml
1 cup quick-cooking oats	240 ml
½ teaspoon baking soda	2 ml
¾ cup (1½ sticks) butter, melted	180 ml

Filling:

1 (6 ounce) package chocolate chips	168 g
¾ cup chopped pecans	180 ml
1 (12 ounce) jar caramel ice cream topping	340 g
3 tablespoons flour	45 ml

- Preheat oven to 350° (176° C).

- Use mixer to blend flour, brown sugar, ⅛ teaspoon (.5 ml) salt, oats, baking soda and butter well enough to form crumbs. Pat down two-thirds crumb mixture into 9 x 13-inch (23 x 33 cm) sprayed baking pan and bake for 10 minutes.

- To prepare filling, remove from oven and sprinkle with chocolate chips and pecans. Blend caramel topping with flour and spread over chips and pecans. Sprinkle with remaining crumb mixture and bake for 20 minutes or until golden brown. Chill for 2 hours before cutting into squares.

BAKE SALE TIP:

If you bake these in a 9 x 13-inch (23 x 33 cm) foil baking pan you can cut into squares and leave in the pan for the sale. Cover with plastic wrap and transport on a metal baking sheet to keep top from cracking.

Kid's Delight

*These are so easy you could make an
extra batch, cut them in small pieces and
pass them out as "appetizers" for the bake sale.*

¼ cup (½ stick) butter	60 ml
1 (10 ounce) package marshmallows	280 g
6 cups cocoa-rice cereal	1.5 L
½ cup miniature chocolate chips	120 ml
½ cup fruit-flavored Skittles®	120 ml

• In large saucepan, over low heat, melt butter and marshmallows. Stir constantly and mix until marshmallows melt. Remove from heat and stir in rice cereal, chocolate chips and Skittles®.

• Spoon into 9 x 13-inch (23 x 33 cm) sprayed baking pan. Use spatula to level cereal mixture. When cool, cut into squares.

BAKE SALE TIP:

One little square of these is never enough, so cut one pan of these in 2 x 2-inch (5 x 5 cm) squares and wrap in separate pieces of light colored plastic wrap. They will look pretty on plastic platter with a white doily and can be sold individually.

Pumpkin Crunch

This is great served warm or cold.

1 (16 ounce) can pumpkin	.5 kg
1 cup sugar	240 ml
1 tablespoon pumpkin pie spice	15 ml
3 eggs	
1 (12 ounce) can evaporated milk	340 g
1 (18 ounce) yellow cake mix	510 g
½ cup (1 stick) butter, melted	120 ml
1 cup chopped pecans	240 ml

- Preheat oven to 350° (176° C).

- In mixing bowl, combine pumpkin, sugar, pie spice, eggs, ½ teaspoon (2 ml) salt and evaporated milk and beat well.

- Pour into 9 x 13-inch (23 x 33 cm) sprayed, floured foil baking pan.

- Mix cake mix, melted butter and pecans to make crumbly mixture. Spoon cake mixture over pumpkin mixture. Bake for 35 to 40 minutes.

- Cut into squares.

Strawberry Crumbles

2¼ cups baking mix	540 ml
1 cup quick-cooking oats	240 ml
1¼ cups packed brown sugar	300 ml
½ cup (1 stick) butter, softened	120 ml
½ cup chopped pecans	120 ml
1 cup strawberry preserves	240 ml

- Preheat oven to 375° (190° C).

- Mix baking mix, oats and brown sugar. Cut in butter with pastry blender until mixture crumbles.

- Stir in chopped pecans and press half this mixture in bottom of 9 x 13-inch (23 x 33 cm) sprayed baking pan. Spread strawberry preserves over crumbly mixture to within ¼-inch (.6 cm) of edges.

- Sprinkle remaining crumbly mixture over top and gently press into fruit. Bake for 30 minutes or until light brown. Cool and cut into bars.

BAKE SALE TIP:

When a dessert bakes in a 9-inch (23 cm) pan, it doesn't look like very much, so always place the bars on doily-lined plastic plate. You could also add some Skittles® around the bars. There are many red ones in 1 (16 ounce/.5 kg) package, so for this recipe scatter the red ones around bars.

Sweet Memories

¾ cup whipping cream	180 ml
1 (12 ounce) package milk chocolate chips	340 g
4 cups multi-colored miniature marshmallows	1 L
1 (7.5 ounce) package chocolate-covered graham crackers	210 g

- Place whipping cream in large saucepan and heat on medium-low heat.

- Add chocolate chips and stir until they melt. Remove from heat. Add marshmallows and stir to coat.

- Break up graham crackers into bite-size pieces (do not crush) and gently stir into cream-marshmallow mixture.

- Spread into 9-inch (23 cm) foil-lined square pan. Refrigerate at least 3 hours or until firm. Cut into squares to serve.

White Chocolate Salties

8 (2 ounce) squares white chocolate bars	8 (57 g)
1 tablespoon shortening	15 ml
1 cup salted honey-roasted peanuts	240 ml
3 cups thin pretzel sticks, broken up	710 ml

- Place white chocolate bars and shortening in large saucepan. On low heat, cook, stirring constantly, until candy melts. Remove from heat, add peanuts and pretzels and stir until chocolate mixture coats peanuts and pretzels. Drop by tablespoonfuls onto wax paper. Chill 20 minutes before storing.

Sugar-Rush Candies

Santa's Favorite Fudge

4½ cups sugar	1 L
1 (12 ounce) can evaporated milk	340 g
1 cup (2 sticks) butter	240 ml
3 (6 ounce) packages chocolate chips	3 (168 g)
1 tablespoon vanilla	15 ml
1½ cups chopped pecans	360 ml

- Bring sugar and milk to rolling boil (boiling that cannot be stirred down). Boil for exactly 6 minutes, stirring constantly.

- Remove from heat, add butter and chocolate chips and stir until they melt. Add vanilla and pecans and stir well.

- Pour into 9 x 13-inch (23 x 33 cm) sprayed dish and let stand 6 hours to overnight before cutting.

- Store in airtight container or plastic plate wrapped in clear plastic wrap.

BAKE SALE TIP:

Include a thank-you note with each purchase. Remind visitors that community events, such as yours, are important.

Peanut Butter Fudge

4 cups sugar	1 L
2 (5 ounce) cans evaporated milk	2 (143 g)
1 cup (2 sticks) butter	240 ml
1¾ cups peanut butter chips	420 ml
1 (7 ounce) jar marshmallow creme	198 g
1 cup finely chopped honey-roasted peanuts	240 ml
1 teaspoon vanilla	5 ml

• Line 8-inch (20 cm) baking pan with foil extending over edges.

• In large saucepan, place sugar, evaporated milk and butter and cook, stirring constantly, over medium-high heat to soft-ball stage, about 12 minutes or 236° (110° C) with candy thermometer.

• Remove from heat and stir in peanut butter chips, marshmallow creme, peanuts and vanilla and stir until chips melt. Spread into sprayed pan and score into 36 squares while still warm. When firm, cut into squares, cool completely and wrap individually or in small batches in plastic wrap.

Minute Fudge

1 (18 ounce) package semi-sweet
  chocolate chips   510 g
1 (14 ounce) can sweetened condensed milk 396 g
¾ cup chopped walnuts   180 ml
1½ teaspoons vanilla   7 ml

- In heavy saucepan over low heat, combine chocolate
  chips and sweetened condensed milk. Cook, stirring
  constantly, until chips melt. Stir in walnuts, vanilla
  and dash of salt.

- Pour into 9-inch (23 cm) sprayed foil-lined square pan
  and chill at least 2 hours. Turn fudge onto cutting
  board and peel away foil. Cut into squares.

Easy Peanut Butter Fudge

1 (12 ounce) jar chunky peanut butter   340 g
1 (12 ounce) package milk chocolate chips 340 g
1 (14 ounce) can sweetened condensed milk 396 g
1 cup chopped pecans   240 ml

- Melt peanut butter and chocolate chips in saucepan.
  Add sweetened condensed milk and heat, just until
  mixture is bubbly.

- Add pecans and mix well. Pour into 9 x 9-inch
  (23 x 23 cm) sprayed dish. Cool before cutting into
  squares.

Diamond Fudge

1 (6 ounce) package semi-sweet	
chocolate chips	168 g
1 cup creamy peanut butter	240 ml
½ cup (1 stick) butter	120 ml
1 cup powdered sugar	240 ml

- Cook chocolate chips, peanut butter and butter in saucepan over low heat. Stir constantly, just until mixture melts and is smooth.

- Remove from heat, add powdered sugar and stir until smooth.

- Spoon into buttered 8-inch (20 cm) square pan and chill until firm. Let stand 10 minutes at room temperature before cutting into squares. Store in refrigerator.

White Chocolate Fudge

This is a little different slant to fudge.
It's really creamy and good!

1 (8 ounce) package cream cheese, softened	227 g
4 cups powdered sugar	1 L
1½ teaspoons vanilla extract	7 ml
12 ounces almond bark, melted	340 g
¾ cup chopped pecans	180 ml

- Beat cream cheese at medium speed with mixer until smooth, gradually add sugar and vanilla and beat ··· ·

- Stir in melted almond bark and pecans 8-inch (20 cm) sprayed square pan.

- Chill until firm and cut into small square

Chocolate Truffles

¾ cup (1½ sticks) butter	180 ml
¾ cup cocoa	180 ml
1 (14 ounce) can sweetened condensed milk	396 g
3 tablespoons rum	45 ml
1 cup finely chopped pecans, divided	240 ml

- Melt butter in small saucepan and stir in cocoa until smooth. (Make sure all lumps are gone.)

- Stir constantly while slowly adding sweetened condensed milk.

- Continue to stir and cook mixture until it thickens and is smooth and shiny, about 5 minutes.

- Remove from heat and stir in rum and ¾ cup (180 ml) pecans.

- Pour into baking pan and chill for several hours until mixture is firm enough to shape.

- Remove mixture from pan by tablespoons and shape into 1-inch (2.5 cm) balls.

- Roll balls in remaining chopped pecans, place on plate and chill several more hours before serving.

Cracker-Candy Bites

2¾ cups round buttery crackers	660 ml
¾ cup (1½ sticks) butter	180 ml
2 cups packed brown sugar	480 ml
1 (12 ounce) package milk chocolate chips	340 g

- Preheat oven to 350° (176° C).

- Place crackers in 9 x 13-inch (23 x 33 cm) sprayed baking dish.

- In saucepan, combine butter and brown sugar and bring to a boil. Boil 3 minutes, stir constantly and pour over crackers.

- Bake for 5 minutes and TURN OVEN OFF.

- Sprinkle chocolate chips over cracker mixture. Return to oven and let stand about 5 minutes or until chocolate melts.

- Remove from oven and spread chocolate evenly over cracker mixture. Cool and break into pieces.

Divinity

2½ cups sugar	600 ml
½ cup light corn syrup	120 ml
2 egg whites	
1 teaspoon vanilla	5 ml
1 cup chopped pecans	5 ml

- Mix sugar, corn syrup, ½ cup (120 ml) water and ¼ teaspoon (1 ml) salt in 2-quart (2 L) saucepan. Cook over medium heat, stirring constantly, until mixture comes to a boil.

- Reduce heat, cook without stirring, until temperature reaches 265° (130° C) or until small amount of syrup forms a ball in cold water. (It holds its shape, yet pliable.)

- Just before temperature reaches 265° (130° C), beat egg whites in large bowl until stiff peaks form when beater raises.

- Beat constantly on high speed and very slowly pour hot syrup over egg whites.

- Continue beating until small amount holds soft peaks when dropped from a spoon. Mix in vanilla and pecans. Work fast and drop by teaspoonfuls onto wax paper.

  TIP: It is best to make divinity on a sunny day. Candy won't set on a damp day.

Macadamia Candy

This is good, good, good!

2 (3 ounce) jars macadamia nuts	2 (84 g)
1 (20 ounce) package white almond bark	567 g
¾ cup flaked coconut	180 ml

- Heat dry skillet over medium heat, toast nuts until slightly golden and set aside.

- In double boiler, melt white almond bark. (If you don't have a double boiler, just put water in a large skillet, heat to boiling and place white almond bark in saucepan into skillet of hot water.)

- As soon as almond bark melts, pour in macadamia nuts and coconut and stir well.

- Place piece of wax paper on cookie sheet, pour candy on wax paper and spread out.

- Chill 30 minutes to set. Break into pieces to serve.

Patience

This is a special family recipe!

1 cup milk	240 ml
3 cups sugar, divided	710 ml
2 tablespoons butter	30 ml
1 teaspoon vanilla	5 ml
1 cup chopped pecans	240 ml

- Heat milk and 2 cups (480 ml) sugar in saucepan. (Do not scorch milk.)

- Pour remaining sugar in skillet, heat and stir until sugar melts (caramelizes).

- Combine caramelized sugar with milk mixture and cook until small drops form softballs in cold water.

- Add butter and vanilla. Cool slightly in pan. Beat until candy is dull and add pecans. Pour into buttered pan or drop by teaspoonfuls.

  TIP: It is best to make this on a sunny day. Candy won't set on a damp day.

Date-Nut Loaf Candy

6 cups sugar	1.5 L
1 (12 ounce) can evaporated milk	340 g
½ cup light corn syrup	120 ml
1 cup (2 sticks) butter	240 ml
2 (8 ounce) boxes chopped dates	2 (227 g)
3 cups chopped pecans or English walnuts	710 ml
1 tablespoon vanilla	15 ml

- In large saucepan, stir constantly with wooden spoon and cook sugar, milk, corn syrup and butter until it boils about 5 minutes. Add dates and cook until it forms soft-ball in cup of cold water.

- Take candy off heat and beat until it begins to get thick. Add pecans and vanilla and stir until real thick. Spoon it onto a wet cup towel to make a roll. This will make 2 rolls of candy. Let it stay wrapped until it is firm enough to slice.

Creamy Pralines

2¼ cups sugar	540 ml
1 (3 ounce) can evaporated milk	84 g
½ cup light corn syrup	120 ml
¼ teaspoon baking soda	1 ml
¼ cup (½ stick) butter	5 ml
1 teaspoon vanilla	5 ml
2 cups pecans	480 ml

• In double boiler, combine sugar, evaporated milk, corn syrup and baking soda. Cook, stirring constantly, until balls form when dropped into cup of cold water or until it reaches soft-ball stage on candy thermometer. This will take about 15 minutes.

• Remove from heat, add butter, vanilla and pecans and beat until it is stiff enough to keep its shape when dropped on wax paper.

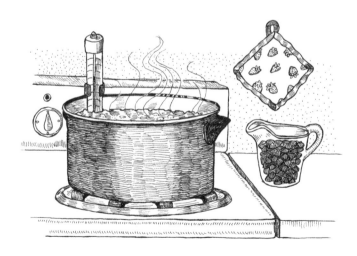

Pecan Toffee

This delightful candy is very easy to make.

1 cup (2 sticks) butter	240 ml
1 cup firmly packed brown sugar	240 ml
1 cup coarsely chopped pecans	240 ml
2 (3.5 ounce) milk chocolate bars	2 (100 g)

- Place butter in saucepan and melt over medium-high heat. Stir in brown sugar and bring to a boil.

- Boil sugar mixture for 12 minutes, stirring constantly. Occasionally wash down sides of pan with wet pastry brush.

- Remove pan from heat and quickly stir in pecans.

- Pour toffee mixture into 9 x 13-inch (23 x 33 cm) sprayed baking pan and use buttered spatula to spread evenly.

- Place chocolate bars on top of toffee; when chocolate melts, spread chocolate evenly over surface. Cool and cut into pieces.

Red Peanut Patties

3 cups sugar   710 ml
1 cup light corn syrup   240 ml
1 pound (3½ cups) raw Spanish peanuts   .5 kg/830 ml
6 drops red food coloring
¼ cup (½ stick) butter   60 ml

- In heavy saucepan, combine sugar, 1 cup (240 ml) water, corn syrup, bring to a boil and stir constantly. Add peanuts and coloring and cook until hard-ball stage 250° (121° C) on candy thermometer.

- Remove from heat, add butter and a pinch of salt and beat until mixture thickens. Pour just enough to make ½-inch (1.2 cm) patty into sprayed muffin pans. Allow to cool completely.

BAKE SALE TIP:

Wrap patties individually with plastic wrap, but beware, your buyers will start eating them before they even get out the door.

Peanut Brittle

2 cups sugar	480 ml
½ cup light corn syrup	120 ml
2 cups dry-roasted peanuts	480 ml
1 tablespoon butter	15 ml
1 teaspoon baking soda	5 ml

- Combine sugar and corn syrup in saucepan. Cook over low heat and stir constantly until sugar dissolves.

- Cover and cook over medium heat another 2 minutes.

- Uncover, add peanuts and cook, stirring occasionally, to hard-crack stage 300° (148° C).

- Stir quickly in butter and baking soda, pour into sprayed jelly-roll pan and spread thinly. Cool and break into pieces.

Nutty Haystacks

1 pound candy orange slices, chopped	.5 kg
2 cups flaked coconut	480 ml
2 cups chopped pecans	480 ml
1 (14 ounce) can sweetened condensed milk	396 g
2 cups powdered sugar	480 ml

- Preheat oven to 350° (176° C). Place orange slices, coconut, pecans and sweetened condensed milk in baking dish and bake for 12 minutes or until bubbly. Add powdered sugar and mix well. Drop by teaspoonfuls on wax paper.

Sure-Selling Snacks

Crispy Fudge Treats

6 cups rice crispy cereal	1.5 L
¾ cup powdered sugar	180 ml
1¾ cups semi-sweet chocolate chips	420 ml
½ cup light corn syrup	120 ml
⅓ cup (⅔ stick) butter	80 ml
2 teaspoons vanilla	10 ml

- Combine cereal and sugar in large bowl and set aside.

- Place chocolate chips, corn syrup and butter in 1-quart (1 L) microwave-safe dish.

- Microwave uncovered on HIGH for about 1 minute, add vanilla and stir until smooth. Pour over cereal mixture and mix well.

- Spoon into 9 x 13-inch (23 x 33 cm) sprayed pan, chill for 30 minutes and cut into squares.

Surprise Chocolates

2 pounds white chocolate or almond bark	1 kg
2 cups Spanish peanuts	480 ml
2 cups small pretzel sticks, broken	480 ml

- Melt chocolate in double boiler. Stir in peanuts and pretzels.

- Drop by teaspoonfuls onto wax paper. (Work fast because mixture hardens quickly.)

- Freeze for 1 hour. Store at room temperature.

Crispy-Crunchy Treats

2 (10 ounce) packages marshmallows	2 (280 g)
½ cup (1 stick) butter	120 ml
12 cups rice crispy cereal	3 L
1 cup coarsely chopped walnuts, toasted	240 ml

- In large saucepan, combine marshmallows and butter. Cook on low-medium heat and stir several times until marshmallows melt. Stir in half cereal and walnuts until the butter mixture covers them. Stir in remaining cereal and walnuts.

- Transfer mixture to 9 x 13-inch (23 x 33 cm) sprayed baking dish and spread evenly with back of large buttered spoon or spatula. Cool completely. Cut into large squares then into triangles.

BAKE SALE TIP:

If you want to make these a really special treat, melt 1 (12 ounce /340 g) package semi-sweet chocolate chips with 1 tablespoon (15 ml) shortening. Dip 1 end of triangle into chocolate and let dry.

Oat Munchies

This is great for munching!

1 (16 ounce) package oat squares cereal	.5 kg
2 cups whole pecans	480 ml
½ cup corn syrup	120 ml
½ cup packed brown sugar	120 ml
¼ cup (½ stick) butter	60 ml
1 teaspoon vanilla	5 ml
½ teaspoon baking soda	2 ml

- Preheat oven to 250° (121° C).

- Combine cereal and pecans in 9 x 13-inch (23 x 33 cm) baking pan and set aside.

- Combine corn syrup, brown sugar and butter in 2-cup (480 ml) bowl. Microwave on HIGH 1½ minutes, stir and turn bowl. Microwave on HIGH about 1 minute or until boiling.

- Stir in vanilla and baking soda. Pour over cereal mixture and stir well to coat evenly.

- Bake for 1 hour and stir every 20 minutes. Spread on baking sheet to cool.

Orange Fingers

3¼ cups vanilla wafer crumbs	770 ml
1 (16 ounce) box powdered sugar	.5 kg
2 cups chopped pecans	480 ml
1 (16 ounce) can frozen orange juice concentrate, thawed	.5 kg
½ cup (1 stick) butter, melted	120 ml
1 cup flaked coconut	240 ml

• Combine vanilla wafer crumbs, powdered sugar and pecans and mix well. Stir in orange juice and butter.

• Shape into 2-inch (5 cm) fingers, roll in coconut and chill.

Chex® Buddies

9 cups Chex® cereal	2 L
1 cup chocolate chips	240 ml
½ cup peanut butter	120 ml
¼ cup ½ stick) butter	60 ml
¼ teaspoon vanilla	1 ml
1½ cups powder sugar	360 ml

• Combine cereal and chips. Melt peanut butter, butter and vanilla; pour over cereal.

• Place powdered sugar in plastic bag and add cereal mixture. Shake bag to coat cereal.

• Spread on cookie sheet for 2 or 3 hours and store in airtight container.

Salty-Sweet Skittle Diddles

1 (8 ounce) package cheddar cheese pretzel sandwiches	227 g
1 (16 ounce) package fruit-flavored Skittles®	.5 kg
2 cups sour dough pretzel nibblers	480 ml
4 (1 ounce) cubes white chocolate, broken up	4 (28 g)
1 (12 ounce) can mixed nuts	340 g
1 (6 ounce) package dried, sweetened pineapple	168 g

• Combine all ingredients.

Zorro's Nutty Snacks

2 cups jalapeno pretzel pieces	480 ml
1 (12 ounce) can whole cashew	340 g
1 (8 ounce) package vanilla-yogurt raisins	227 g
2 cups chocolate pretzel dips	480 ml
1 (7 ounce) package maple-nut goodies	198 g
1 (16 ounce) jar honey-roasted peanuts	.5 kg

• Combine all ingredients.

Spiced Pecans

You can't eat just one!

2 cups sugar	480 ml
2 teaspoons cinnamon	10 ml
1 teaspoon ground nutmeg	5 ml
½ teaspoon ground cloves	2 ml
4 cups pecan halves	1 L

- Combine sugar, cinnamon, nutmeg, cloves, ½ cup (120 ml) water and ¼ teaspoon (1 ml) salt.

- Mix well, cover with wax paper and microwave on HIGH for 4 minutes. Stir and microwave another 4 minutes.

- Add pecans, quickly mix well and spread on wax paper to cool.

- Break apart and store in covered container.

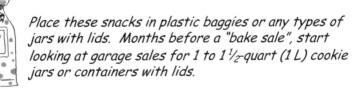

BAKE SALE TIP:

Place these snacks in plastic baggies or any types of jars with lids. Months before a "bake sale", start looking at garage sales for 1 to 1½-quart (1 L) cookie jars or containers with lids.

I found several plastic 1 to 2-quart (1 L) containers at discount stores and even some large water glasses that could be filled, covered with a colorful plastic wrap and tied with a fancy little bow. I also found 4 x 9-inch (10 x 23 cm) plastic bags that come with a silver twist tie. Use small container to package these snacks.

Roasted Mixed Nuts

1 pound mixed nuts	.5 kg
¼ cup maple syrup	60 ml
2 tablespoons brown sugar	30 ml
1 (1 ounce) packet dry ranch-style salad dressing mix	28 g

- Preheat oven to 300° (148° C).

- In bowl, combine nuts and maple syrup and mix well.

- Sprinkle with brown sugar and salad dressing mix and stir gently to coat.

- Spread in 10 x 15-inch (25 x 38 cm) sprayed baking pan.

- Bake for 25 minutes or until light brown. Cool.

Haystacks

1 (12 ounce) package butterscotch chips	340 g
1 cup salted peanuts	240 ml
1½ cups chow mein noodles	360 ml

- Melt butterscotch chips in top of double boiler. Remove from heat and stir in peanuts and noodles.

- Drop by teaspoonfuls on wax paper.

- Cool and store in airtight container.

Tumbleweeds

1 (12 ounce) can salted peanuts	340 g
1 (7 ounce) can potato sticks, broken up	198 g
3 cups butterscotch chips	710 ml
3 tablespoons peanut butter	45 ml

- Combine peanuts and potato sticks in bowl and set aside.

- In microwave, heat butterscotch chips and peanut butter at 70% for 1 to 2 minutes or until they melt and stir every 30 seconds. Add to peanut mixture and stir to coat evenly.

- Drop by rounded tablespoonfuls onto wax paper-lined baking sheet. Refrigerate until set, about 10 minutes.

Chocolate-Peanut Butter Drops

1 cup sugar	240 ml
½ cup light corn syrup	120 ml
¼ cup honey	60 ml
1½ cups chunky peanut butter	360 ml
4 cups chocolate-flavored frosted corn puff cereal	1 L

- Combine sugar, corn syrup and honey in large heavy pan. Bring to a boil and stir constantly.

- Remove from heat, add peanut butter and stir until it blends.

- Stir in cereal and drop by tablespoonfuls onto wax paper. Cool.

Chocolate-Peanut Clusters

1 cup semi-sweet chocolate chips	240 ml
½ cup premier white chocolate chips	120 ml
1 tablespoon shortening	15 ml
1 (11 ounce) package lightly salted peanuts, divided	312 g

- Microwave chocolate chips, white chocolate chips and shortening on HIGH for 1 to 2 minutes or until chips melt.

- Stir until chips blend and mixture is smooth.

- Set aside ¼ cup (60 ml) peanuts for topping.

- Pour remaining peanuts into chocolate mixture and mix well.

- Drop by teaspoonfuls into 1-inch (2.5 cm) clusters on baking sheet. Put remaining peanuts on top of each cluster.

- Chill until clusters are firm and store in airtight container.

Butterscotch Peanuts

1 (12 ounce) package butterscotch chips	340 g
2 cups chow mein noodles	480 ml
1 cup dry roasted peanuts	240 ml

- In saucepan, heat butterscotch chips over low heat until they melt completely.

- Add noodles and peanuts and stir until butterscotch covers each piece.

- Drop from spoon onto wax paper. Cool and store in airtight container.

Holiday Mix Snacks

2 cups pistachio nuts	480 ml
2 cups honey-roasted peanuts	480 ml
1 (6 ounce) package dried, sweetened pineapple	168 g
1 (12 ounce) package white chocolate chips	340 g
1 (6 ounce) package Craisins® (dried cranberries)	168 g

- Combine all ingredients and store in airtight containers.

Saturday Night Nibblers

1 (12 ounce) package chocolate-covered peanuts	340 g
1 (8 ounce) package vanilla-yogurt raisins	227 g
1 (12 ounce) package M&M's®	340 g
1 cup slivered almonds, toasted	240 ml
1 (12 ounce) can whole cashews	340 g

- Combine all ingredients and store in airtight containers.

BAKE SALE TIP:

For the bake sale, place nibblers in pint jars with lids. Cut colorful fabrics into 6-inch (15 cm) rounds, place over lid and tie with a narrow, colorful ribbon. Another way to package these snacks is to buy jar lids that have a separate ring. Place fabric on top and screw lid around jar.

Another easy way to package these snacks is to place mixtures in muffin cups with silver on the outside. Cut a large square of plastic wrap, place muffin cups in middle, bring clear plastic wrap up and tie with colorful ribbon. This size will sell for a lot less, but people will buy several to share or eat immediately.

Crazy Cocoa Crisps

1 (24 ounce) package white almond bark	680 g
2¼ cups cocoa crispy rice cereal	540 ml
2 cups dry-roasted peanuts	480 ml

- Place almond bark in double boiler and heat, while stirring constantly, until bark melts.

- Stir in cereal and peanuts and drop by teaspoonfuls on baking sheet. Store in airtight containers.

Christmas Caramel Corn

8 cups popped popcorn	1.8 L
1½ cups whole almonds, cashews or pecans	360 ml
1 (16 ounce) package dried fruit bits	.5 kg
1 cup packed brown sugar	240 ml
½ cup sugar	120 ml
⅔ cup butter	160 ml
⅓ cup light corn syrup	80 ml
½ teaspoon baking soda	2 ml
½ teaspoon vanilla	2 ml

- Preheat oven to 300° (148° C).

- Place popcorn, nuts and dried fruit on baking sheet. In heavy saucepan, combine both sugars, butter and syrup, bring to a boil and stir often.

- Continue to cook and to stir about 15 minutes until mixture is golden brown. Remove from heat, stir in baking soda and vanilla and pour over popcorn mixture. Stir gently to cover popcorn, nuts and fruit.

- Bake for 15 minutes, stir and continue baking another 5 minutes. Transfer to foil and cool thoroughly. Break up and store in airtight container.

BAKE SALE TIP:

I bought a package of 5 deep square plastic containers with lids at a discount store for $1. One of these containers, which holds 5 cups (1.3 L), would be a good, inexpensive way to display these munchies.

Goody Bag

Caramel Crunch

½ cup firmly packed brown sugar	120 ml
½ cup light corn syrup	120 ml
4 tablespoons (½ stick) butter	60 ml
6 cups crispy corn cereal squares	1.5 L
2 cups peanuts	480 ml

- Preheat oven to 250° (121° C).

- In large saucepan, heat sugar, syrup and butter. Stir constantly until sugar and butter melt.

- Add cereal and peanuts and stir until butter mixture coats cereal and peanuts.

- Spread mixture on lightly sprayed cookie sheet and bake for 30 minutes. Stir occasionally while baking.

- Cool and store in airtight container.

Popcorn Balls

1 cup sugar	240 ml
⅓ cup light corn syrup	80 ml
1 teaspoon vinegar	5 ml
Green or red food coloring, optional	
½ teaspoon vanilla	2 ml
3 quarts popped popcorn	3 L

- Boil sugar, ½ cup (120 ml) water, corn syrup, ½ teaspoon (2 ml) salt and vinegar until hard-ball stage.

- Add desired food coloring and vanilla and stir well. Pour over popcorn.

- Butter hands lightly and shape into balls. Wrap each in plastic wrap.

No-Bake Kids Treats

¼ cup (½ stick) butter	60 ml
1 (10 ounce) package marshmallows	280 g
½ cup M&M's®	120 ml
About 7 cups rice crispy cereal	1.6 L
12 wooden popsicle sticks	
1 (12 ounce) package milk chocolate chips	340 g

- In large saucepan, melt butter and marshmallows over low heat, stirring constantly until marshmallows melt. Remove from heat and stir in M&M's® and cereal until butter mixture covers them.

- Let mixture cool until it is warm but comfortable enough to handle with your fingers. Lightly butter your hands and shape treats into 12 balls. Push 1 popsicle stick into each ball. Set aside to cool.

- In small saucepan, melt chocolate chips and dip balls into chocolate while holding the stick. Place coated treats on wax paper-lined tray to cool.

Chocolate-Dipped Stuffed Dates

*Although it may seem that adding anything
at all to these luscious dates is "gilding the lily"
because they are fabulous just by themselves ,the
addition of nuts and chocolate makes this a truly exquisite treat.*

24 Medjool dates
24 walnut halves
3 ounces semi-sweet chocolate, melted   84 g

- With paring knife, slice each date down one side and remove pit. Insert walnut half.

- Dip bottom half of each stuffed date in melted chocolate and place on wax paper or foil to set.

  TIP: If you cut from 1 end of the date toward the stem end, the pit may be easily pushed out by the knife as you slice. This date recipe makes a great finger food for a party because it is easy and neat to eat.

Wine Jelly

This is great served with pork!

2 cups white wine   480 ml
½ cup lime juice   120 ml
1 (1.5 ounce) box fruit pectin   45 g
4¼ cups sugar   1 L

- In saucepan large enough for jelly to bubble up while cooking, combine wine, ½ cup (120 ml) water and lime juice. Bring to boiling point and stir in fruit pectin.

- Add sugar, bring to a boil and boil for 1 minute. Skim foam off jelly then pour into jelly jars. Seal with paraffin.

  TIP: This is a great appetizer when you pour over cream cheese and spread it on a cracker.

EQUIVALENTS

FOOD	QUANTITY	YIELD
Almonds, sliced	2¼ ounces (65 g)	½ cup (125 ml)
Almonds, slivered	2 ounces (57 g)	⅓ cup (80 ml)
Apple pie filling	21-ounce can (598 g)	2⅓ cups (580 ml)
Apples, fresh	1 medium	¾ cup chopped (180 ml); 1 cup diced or sliced (250 ml)
Apples, fresh	1 pound (454 g)	3 medium; 2½ cups peeled (750 ml), diced or sliced; 3 cups unpeeled (750 ml), diced or sliced
Apple slices, canned	20-ounce can (570 g)	2 drained
Apricots, canned	16-ounce can (454 g)	2 cups drained halves (500 ml); 6 to 8 whole
Apricots, dried	6-ounce package (170 g) 2 cups cooked (500 ml)	1 cup dried (250 ml);
Apricots, fresh	2 medium	½ cup sliced (125 ml)
Apricots, fresh	1 pound (454 g)	2 cups halves or slices (500 ml); 8 to 12 medium
Baking powder	7-ounce can (198 g)	1¼ cups (310 ml)
Baking soda	16-ounce box (454 g)	2⅓ cups (580 ml)
Bananas, dried, sliced	1 pound (454 g)	4 to 4½ cups (1 L to 1 L 125 mL)

EQUIVALENTS

FOOD	QUANTITY	YIELD
Bananas, fresh	1 medium	1 cup sliced (250 ml)
Bananas, fresh	1 pound (454 g)	3 small or large; 1½ cups mashed (375 ml); 2 cups sliced (500 ml)
Bisquick	40-ounce box (1.13 kg)	12 cups (3 L)
Blueberries, canned	15-ounce can (438 g)	1½ cups (375 ml)
Blueberries, fresh or frozen	1 pound (454 g)	3½ cups (875 ml); makes 1 (9 inch) pie (23 cm)
Blueberry pie filling	21-ounce can (598 g)	2⅓ cups (580 ml)
Butter	2 tablespoons (30 ml)	"the size of a walnut"
Butter	¼-pound stick (115 g)	½ cup (125 ml); 8 tbsp.; 1 stick; 12 to 16 pats; ⅓ cup clarified butter (80 ml)
Butter	½ pound (228 g)	25 servings
Butter	1 pound (454 g)	2 cups; 4 sticks (500 ml)
Butter, soft	8-ounce tub (228 g)	1 cup (250 ml)
Butter, whipped	1 pound (454 g)	3 cups (750 ml)
Butterscotch morsels	12-ounce package (340 g)	2 cups (500 ml)

EQUIVALENTS

FOOD	QUANTITY	YIELD
Cake mix	18-ounce box (520 g)	5 to 6 cups batter (1.5 L); 2 (9-inch round) layers (23 cm); 2 (8-inch square) layers (20 cm); 1 (13 x 9 x 2 inch) cake (33 x 23 cm); 1 cartoon character cake; 24 cupcakes
Cake, sheet (9 x 13 inch)	1½ cakes	25 servings
Cake, two layer (9 inch)	2 to 2½ cakes	25 servings
Cherries, canned, tart	16-ounce pitted (454 g)	1½ cups drained (375 ml)
Cherries, dried, tart	3-ounce package (85 g)	½ cup (125 ml)
Cherries, fresh, sweet	1-pound unpitted (454 g)	1 quart (1 L); 1¾ cups (430 ml)
Cherries, frozen, tart	1-pound pitted (454 g)	2 cups (500 ml)
Cherry pie filling	21-ounce can (598 g)	2⅓ cups (580 ml)
Chocolate, bar or square	1 ounce (28 g) chopped or grated	3 tablespoons (45 ml)
Chocolate, bar or square	9 ounces (240 g)	1⅝ cups chopped or grated (435 ml); 1 cup (250 ml)

EQUIVALENTS

FOOD	QUANTITY	YIELD
Melted chocolate, unsweetened	1 ounce (28 g)	1 square; 4 tablespoons grated (60 ml)
Chocolate, unsweetened	1 ounce (28 g)	1 envelope liquid
Chocolate bits, M&M's	12-ounce package (340 g)	1½ cups (375 ml)
Chocolate kisses (mini)	10-ounce package (284 g)	209 pieces
Chocolate morsels	12-ounce package (340 g)	2 cups (500 ml)
Chocolate wafers	20 wafers	1 cup fine crumbs (250 ml)
Cinnamon, ground	1 ounce (28 g)	4 tablespoons (60 ml)
Cinnamon, stick	1-inch part of stick	1 teaspoon ground (5 ml)
Cocoa, baking	8-ounce tin	2⅔ cups (660 ml)
Coconut, flaked	3½-ounce can (100 g)	1¼ cups (310 ml)
Coconut, flaked	7-ounce package (198 g)	2½ cups (625 ml)
Coconut, flaked	14-ounce package (420 g)	5⅓ cups (1 L, 330 ml)
Coconut, fresh	1 pound (454 g)	1 medium; 3 cups grated or chopped (750 ml)
Crackers, graham	15 (2½-inch square)	1 cup fine crumbs (250 ml)
Crackers, graham, crumbs	3¾ cups (930 ml); 13½-ounce box (460 g)	makes 3 pie shells

EQUIVALENTS

FOOD	QUANTITY	YIELD
Cranberries, fresh	12-ounce package (340 g)	3 cups (750 ml)
Cranberries, fresh	1-pound package (454 g)	4 cups (1 L); 3 cups cooked sauce (750 ml)
Cream, heavy	½ pint (500 ml)	1 cup unwhipped (250 ml); 2 cups whipped (500 ml)
Cream, heavy (unwhipped)	¾ pint (750 ml)	25 servings
Cream, light (half-and-half)	1 pint (500 ml)	2 cups (500 ml); 16 coffee servings
Cream, whipped, pressurized	7-ounce can (198 g)	1⅞ cups (465 ml)
Cream cheese	3-ounce package (85 g)	⅓ cup (80 ml)
Cream cheese	8-ounce package (228 g)	1 cup (250 ml)
Dates, diced, sugared	1 pound (454 g)	2⅔ cups (680 ml)
Dates, dried, pitted	8-ounce package (228 g)	54 dates; 1¼ cups chopped (310 ml)
Dates, dried with pits	1 pound (454 g)	60 dates; 2½ cups pitted (625 ml)
Flour, all-purpose	5-pound bag (2.5 kg)	20 cups sifted (5 L)
Flour, cake	1 pound (454 g)	4⅛ cups unsifted (1L); 4⅝ cups sifted (1 L, 125 ml)
Flour, self-rising	1 pound (454 g)	4 cups sifted (1 L)

EQUIVALENTS

FOOD	QUANTITY	YIELD
Ginger, crystallized	1 tablespoon (15 ml)	1 teaspoon ground (5 ml)
Ginger, fresh	1 tablespoon chopped (15 ml)	1 teaspoon ground (5 ml)
Ginger, fresh	1½ to 2-inch piece	2 tablespoons grated or chopped (30 ml)
Ginger, ground	½ teaspoon (2 ml)	1 teaspoon fresh chopped (5 ml)
Ginger, ground	1 ounce (28 g)	4 tablespoons (60 ml)
Lemons	1 pound (454 g)	4 to 6 medium; ⅔ to 1 cup juice (160 to 250 ml)
Macadamia nuts	7-ounce jar (198 g)	1½ cups (375 ml)
Marshmallow cream	7-ounce jar (198 g)	2⅛ cups (530 ml)
Milk	1 quart (1 L)	4 cups (1 L)
Milk, sweetened, condensed	14-ounce can (420 g)	1¼ cups (310 ml)
Mincemeat	27-ounce jar (800 g)	2⅔ cups (560 ml)
Mincemeat, condensed	9-ounce box (240 g)	½ cup (125 ml)
Molasses	12-ounce bottle (340 g)	1½ cups (375 ml)
Oreo cookies	12 cookies	1 cup fine crumbs (250 ml)
Oreo cookies	1 pound, 4 ounce package (570 g)	51 cookies

EQUIVALENTS

FOOD	QUANTITY	YIELD
Peaches, canned, sliced	16-ounce can (454 g)	2 to 2½ cups drained (500 to 625 ml)
Peaches, fresh	1 pound (454 g)	3 to 4 medium; 2 cups peeled and sliced or diced (500 ml); 1½ cups pulp (375 ml)
Peaches, fresh	2 pounds (1 kg)	makes 1 (9-inch) pie (23 cm)
Peaches, frozen	10 ounces (284 g)	1 cup slices drained (250 ml); 1¼ cups sliced with juice (310 ml)
Peach pie filling	21-ounce can (300 g)	2⅓ cups (580 ml)
Pecans, chips or pieces	6-ounce package (170 g)	1½ cups (375 ml)
Raisins, seedless	1-pound package (454 g)	3 cups (750 ml)
Raspberries, fresh	1 pint (500 ml)	1¾ cups (430 ml)
Raspberries, frozen	10-ounce package (284 g)	1 cup with syrup (250 ml)
Shortening, solid	1-pound can (454 g)	2½ cups (625 ml)
Shortening, sticks	20-ounce package (570 g)	3 sticks, 1 cup each (250 ml)
Strawberries, fresh	1 cup whole (250 ml)	4 ounces (115 g); ½ cup pureed (125 ml)
Strawberries, fresh	1 pint (500 ml)	2½ cups whole (625 m L); 1¾ cups sliced (430 ml); 1¼ cups pureed (310 ml); 12 large, 24 medium or 36 small

EQUIVALENTS

FOOD	QUANTITY	YIELD
Strawberries, frozen, sliced	10-ounce package (284 g)	1 cup drained (250 ml); 1 ¼ cups with syrup (310 ml)
Strawberries, frozen, whole	20-ounce package (570 g)	4 cups whole (1 L); 2 ¼ cups pureed (560 ml)
Strawberry pie filling	21-ounce can (578 g)	2 ⅓ cups (680 ml)
Sugar, brown	1 pound (454 g)	2 ¼ cups packed (560 ml)
Sugar, confectioners	1 pound (454 g)	3 ¾ cups unsifted (930 ml); 4 ¼ cups sifted (1 L, 60 ml)
Sugar, granulated	1 pound (454 g)	2 ¼ cups (560 ml)
Sugar, granulated	5-pound bag (2.5 kg)	11 ¼ cups (3 L)
Sugar cubes	1-pound box (454 g)	96 cubes
Vanilla extract	1 ounce (28 g)	2 ½ tablespoons (37 ml)
Vanilla wafers	30 wafers	1 cup fine crumbs (250 ml)
Walnuts, halves	7-ounce package (198 g)	1 ¾ cups (430 ml)
Walnuts, pieces	2 ½-ounce package (71 g)	½ cup (125 ml)
Whipped topping, frozen	8-ounce carton (228 g)	3 ½ cups (875 ml)
Whipped topping mix	1.4-ounce package (35 g)	2 cups whipped topping (560 ml)

SUBSTITUTION LIST

IF YOU NEED THIS:
SUBSTITUTE THIS

2 tablespoons (30 ml) almonds, ground (for flavoring):
¼ teaspoon (1 ml) almond extract

1 teaspoon (5 ml) apple pie spice:
½ teaspoon (2 ml) ground cinnamon plus
¼ teaspoon (1 ml) ground nutmeg plus
⅛ teaspoon (.5 ml) ground allspice plus
⅛ teaspoon (.5 ml) ground cardamom

1 teaspoon (5 ml) baking powder, double acting:
¼ teaspoon (1 ml) baking soda plus
½ cup (125 ml) buttermilk
(Reduce other liquid in recipe by ½ cup (125 ml)

2¼ cups (560 ml) biscuit mix:
2 cups (500 ml) flour, sifted with plus
1 tablespoon (15 ml) baking powder
1 teaspoon (5 ml) salt plus
¼ cup (60 ml) shortening (cut in)

1 cup (250 ml) butter (for baking):
⅞ cup (220 ml) shortening plus
½ (2 ml) teaspoon salt

1 cup (250 ml) buttermilk:
1 tablespoon (10 ml) lemon juice or white vinegar plus
⅞ cup (220 ml) plus 1 tablespoon (15 ml) whole milk
(Let stand for 10 minutes.)

1 cup (250 ml) buttermilk (for baking):
1 cup (250 ml) plain yogurt or 1 cup (250 ml) sour cream

6 ounces (170 g) chocolate morsels:
9 tablespoons (135 ml) cocoa powder plus
7 tablespoons (105 ml) sugar plus
3 tablespoons (45 ml) butter

SUBSTITUTION LIST

IF YOU NEED THIS:
        SUBSTITUTE THIS

2 tablespoons (30 ml) almonds, ground (for flavoring):
        ¼ teaspoon (1 ml) almond extract

1 teaspoon (5 ml) apple pie spice:
        ½ teaspoon (2 ml) ground cinnamon plus
        ¼ teaspoon (1 ml) ground nutmeg plus
        ⅛ teaspoon (.5 ml) ground allspice plus
        ⅛ teaspoon (.5 ml) ground cardamom

1 teaspoon (5 ml) baking powder, double acting:
        ¼ teaspoon (1 ml) baking soda plus
        ½ cup (125 ml) buttermilk
        (Reduce other liquid in recipe by ½ cup (125 ml).)

2¼ cups (560 ml) biscuit mix:
        2 cups (500 ml) flour, sifted with plus
        1 tablespoon (15 ml) baking powder
        1 teaspoon (5 ml) salt plus
        ¼ cup (60 ml) shortening (cut in)

1 cup (250 ml) butter (for baking):
        ⅞ cup (220 ml) shortening plus
        ½ (2 ml) teaspoon salt

1 cup (250 ml) buttermilk:
        1 tablespoon (10 ml) lemon juice or white vinegar plus
        ⅞ cup (220 ml) plus 1 tablespoon (15 ml) whole milk
        (Let stand for 10 minutes.)

1 cup (250 ml) buttermilk (for baking):
        1 cup (250 ml) plain yogurt or 1 cup (250 ml) sour cream

6 ounces (170 g) chocolate morsels:
        9 tablespoons (135 ml) cocoa powder plus
        7 tablespoons (105 ml) sugar plus
        3 tablespoons (45 ml) butter

SUBSTITUTION LIST

IF YOU NEED THIS:
          SUBSTITUTE THIS

2 ounces (57 g) chocolate, semisweet:
          ⅓ cup (80 ml) chocolate chips

1 ounce (28 g) chocolate, semisweet:
          ½ ounce (14 g) unsweetened chocolate plus
          1 tablespoon (15 ml) sugar

1 ounce (28 g) chocolate square, unsweetened:
          3½ tablespoons (52 ml) cocoa powder plus
          2 teaspoons (10 ml) butter or shortening

1 cup (250 ml) grated coconut:
          1⅓ (330 ml) cups flaked coconut

1 cup (250 ml) heavy cream (for cooking, not whipping):
          ¾ cup (180 ml) whole milk plus
          ⅓ cup (80 ml) butter

1 cup (250 ml) light cream:
          ½ cup (125 ml) heavy cream plus
          ½ cup (125 ml) whole milk

1 cup (250 ml) light cream (for cooking):
          ⅞ cup (220 ml) whole milk plus
          3 tablespoons (45 ml) butter

1 cup (250 ml) light cream (for cooking):
          1 cup (250 ml) evaporated milk

1 cup (250 ml) cream, whipped, sweetened:
          4 ounces (115 g) whipped topping

1 cup (250 ml) cream, whipped, sweetened:
          1¼ ounces (35 g) dessert topping mix, prepared

1 cup (250 ml) whipping cream:
          ⅔ cup (160 ml) evaporated milk plus
          4 teaspoons (20 ml) lemon juice or vinegar

SUBSTITUTION LIST

IF YOU NEED THIS:
> SUBSTITUTE THIS

2 tablespoons (30 ml) almonds, ground (for flavoring):
> ¼ teaspoon (1 ml) almond extract

1 teaspoon (5 ml) apple pie spice:
> ½ teaspoon (2 ml) ground cinnamon plus
> ¼ teaspoon (1 ml) ground nutmeg plus
> ⅛ teaspoon (.5 ml) ground allspice plus
> ⅛ teaspoon (.5 ml) ground cardamom

1 teaspoon (5 ml) baking powder, double acting:
> ¼ teaspoon (1 ml) baking soda plus
> ½ cup (125 ml) buttermilk
> (Reduce other liquid in recipe by ½ cup (125 ml).)

2¼ cups (560 ml) biscuit mix:
> 2 cups (500 ml) flour, sifted with plus
> 1 tablespoon (15 ml) baking powder
> 1 teaspoon (5 ml) salt plus
> ¼ cup (60 ml) shortening (cut in)

1 cup (250 ml) butter (for baking):
> ⅞ cup (220 ml) shortening plus
> ½ (2 ml) teaspoon salt

1 cup (250 ml) buttermilk:
> 1 tablespoon (10 ml) lemon juice or white vinegar plus
> ⅞ cup (220 ml) plus 1 tablespoon (15 ml) whole milk
> (Let stand for 10 minutes.)

1 cup (250 ml) buttermilk (for baking):
> 1 cup (250 ml) plain yogurt or 1 cup (250 ml) sour cream

6 ounces (170 g) chocolate morsels:
> 9 tablespoons (135 ml) cocoa powder plus
> 7 tablespoons (105 ml) sugar plus
> 3 tablespoons (45 ml) butter

COOKBOOKS PUBLISHED BY COOKBOOK RESOURCES, LLC

The Ultimate Cooking with 4 Ingredients

Easy Cooking with 5 Ingredients

The Best of Cooking with 3 Ingredients

Gourmet Cooking with 5 Ingredients

Healthy Cooking with 4 Ingredients

Diabetic Cooking with 4 Ingredients

4-Ingredient Recipes for 30-Minute Meals

Essential 3-4-5 Ingredient Recipes

The Best 1001 Short, Easy Recipes

Easy Slow Cooker Cookbook

Easy One-Dish Meals

Easy Potluck Recipes

Quick Fixes with Cake Mixes

Casseroles to the Rescue

Easy Casseroles

Italian Family Cookbook

Sunday Night Suppers

365 Easy Meals

365 Easy Chicken Recipes

365 Easy Soups and Stews

I Ain't On No Diet Cookbook

Kitchen Keepsakes/More Kitchen Keepsakes

Old-Fashioned Cookies

Grandmother's Cookies

Mother's Recipes

Recipe Keeper

Cookie Dough Secrets

Gifts for the Cookie Jar

All New Gifts for the Cookie Jar

Gifts in a Pickle Jar

Muffins In A Jar

Brownies In A Jar

Cookie Jar Magic

Easy Desserts

Bake Sale Bestsellers

Quilters' Cooking Companion

Miss Sadie's Southern Cooking

Southern Family Favorites

Classic Tex-Mex and Texas Cooking

Classic Southwest Cooking

The Great Canadian Cookbook

The Best of Lone Star Legacy Cookbook

Cookbook 25 Years

Pass the Plate

Texas Longhorn Cookbook

Trophy Hunters' Wild Game Cookbook

Mealtimes and Memories

Holiday Recipes

Little Taste of Texas

Little Taste of Texas II

Southwest Sizzler

Southwest Ole'

Class Treats

Leaving Home

To Order: **The Big Bake Sale Cookbook**

Please send _____ hardcover copies @ $19.95 (U.S.) each $ _____

Texas residents add sales tax @ $1.65 each $ _____

Plus postage/handling @ $6.00 (1st copy) $ _____

$1.00 (each additional copy) $ _____

Check or Credit Card (Canada-credit card only) Total $ _____

Charge to: ☐ MasterCard. or ☐ VISA

Account # _____

Expiration Date _____

Signature_____

| Mail or Call: |
| Cookbook Resources |
| 541 Doubletree Dr. |
| Highland Village, Texas 75077 |
| Toll Free (866) 229-2665 |
| (972) 317-6404 Fax |

Name _____

Address_____

City_____State_____Zip_____

Telephone (day_____(Evening)_____

To Order: **The Big Bake Sale Cookbook**

Please send _____ hardcover copies @ $19.95 (U.S.) each $ _____

Texas residents add sales tax @ $1.65 each $ _____

Plus postage/handling @ $6.00 (1st copy) $ _____

$1.00 (each additional copy) $ _____

Check or Credit Card (Canada-credit card only) Total $ _____

Charge to: ☐ MasterCard or ☐ VISA

Account # _____

Expiration Date _____

Signature_____

| Mail or Call: |
| Cookbook Resources |
| 541 Doubletree Dr. |
| Highland Village, Texas 75077 |
| Toll Free (866) 229-2665 |
| (972) 317-6404 Fax |

Name _____

Address_____

City_____State_____Zip_____

Telephone (Day)_____(Evening)_____